Beaver Blacker

Brief Sketches of the Parishes of Booterstown and Donnybrook

In the County of Dublin

Beaver Blacker

Brief Sketches of the Parishes of Booterstown and Donnybrook
In the County of Dublin

ISBN/EAN: 9783337013561

Printed in Europe, USA, Canada, Australia, Japan

Cover: Foto ©Andreas Hilbeck / pixelio.de

More available books at **www.hansebooks.com**

Booterstown Church County Dublin

BRIEF SKETCHES

OF THE

Parishes of Booterstown and Donnybrook,

IN

THE COUNTY OF DUBLIN;

WITH

An Appendix, containing Notes and Annals.

BY THE

REV. BEAVER H. BLACKER, A.M.,

Incumbent of Booterstown.

"Attamen andendum est, et veritas investiganda, quam si non omnino assequeremur, tamen proprius ad eam, quam nunc sumus, tandem perveniemus."

DUBLIN:
GEORGE HERBERT, 117, GRAFTON-STREET.
LONDON: BELL AND DALDY, 186, FLEET-STREET.

1860.

PREFACE.

THE substance of these Brief Sketches of the four churches in the parishes of Booterstown and Donnybrook lately appeared in the *Christian Examiner*, under the title of "Sketches of Suburban Churches" (Nos. I.–IV.); and having been carefully revised and enlarged by the writer, they are now produced in a permanent form. A view of Booterstown Church (from the Cross-avenue) is prefixed; but, as it does not convey an exact idea of the adjacent grounds, as they are at present, it is right to mention that many improvements have been effected since the copperplate was engraved; and particularly, that the Right Honourable Sidney Herbert, M.P., in the year 1854, added considerably to the grounds, and made a new and handsome approach from Mount Merrion-avenue. A view of the church on an enlarged scale, with descriptive particulars, has likewise appeared in the *Church of England Magazine*, vol. xlvi. p. 361 (London, 1859).

The writer is indebted for several interesting particulars to the long-continued labours of Mr. D'Alton, who, in his "History of the County of Dublin," "Memoirs of the Archbishops of Dublin," and many other well-known works, has collected together a vast amount of useful information. Some of his statements, however, are not a little tinged with prejudice (*e.g.* in his account of the late Archbishop Magee, whose advancement to almost the highest ecclesiastical dignity in Ireland was justified, in the general opinion, by the eminent service he had performed in vindicating the doctrines of his Church, but who has been held up to public view as a flagrant instance of " arrogant and uncharitable bigotry"); while other statements, perhaps from the want of proper answers to his inquiries, are incorrect, and consequently leave him exposed to critical objections. Thus (to take an instance near home), he states in his "History of the County of Dublin," p. 861, that "the Incumbent [of Booterstown] has also a glebe-house and glebe"—which unfortunately is not the case.

A long and intimate connexion with Donnybrook has enabled the writer to give many particulars of that parish; and having spared neither time nor trouble, he hopes that he will not be found to be very inaccurate in any of his statements. Being indebted to some kind friends for assistance, he takes this opportunity of acknowledging his obligations.

ROKEBY, BLACKROCK, DUBLIN.
1st *December*, 1859.

> "All only for to publish plaine,
> Tyme past, tyme present both;
> That tyme to come, may well retaine,
> Of each good tyme, the troth."
>
> —THOMAS CHURCHYARD.

PARISH OF BOOTERSTOWN.

INCUMBENT.
REV. BEAVER HENRY BLACKER, A.M.

Booterstown Parish Church.

This church, dedicated to St. Philip and St. James, and beautifully situated in the vicinity of Dublin, was consecrated and opened for Divine service on Sunday, 16th May, 1824, by the late Dr. Magee, Archbishop of the diocese (*a*); the site (with the sum of £1,000) having been given by George Augustus Earl of Pembroke (*b*). The parish, which is a portion of the corps of the archdeaconry of Dublin (*c*), had been formed out of the parish of Donnybrook in the year 1821 (*d*); and the patronage is vested in the Archdeacon. The structure, which was designed by Joseph Welland, Esq., and completed at the cost of nearly £5,000 (*e*), is handsome, in the later English style, with a square embattled tower with crocketed pinnacles at the angles, and surmounted by a lofty spire; the walls

(*a*) Notes applicable to the reference-marks will be found in the Appendix.

are strengthened with buttresses terminating in pinnacles, and crowned with an embattled parapet. In the interior, which accommodates about 500, there are monuments to James Digges La Touche (the early and devoted friend of Sunday Schools in Ireland) and Richard Verschoyle, Esqrs. (*f*); and also one to the Rev. R. H. Nixon (*g*), with this appropriate inscription :—

"Erected by the parishioners of Booterstown, to the memory of the Rev. Robert Herbert Nixon, A.M., who died on the 22nd of January, 1857, in the 75th year of his age, having been for 24 years Incumbent of this parish. Humble in his deportment, affectionate and impressive in his teaching, and uncompromising in his testimony to the truth, he strikingly exemplified the mild and attractive graces of the Gospel. 'Blessed are the dead which die in the Lord from henceforth: Yea, saith the Spirit, that they may rest from their labours; and their works do follow them.'—Rev. xiv. 13."

The Rev. James Bulwer was the first Incumbent of the parish; and Robert Alexander, of Seamount (now St. Helen's, the seat of Lord Viscount Gough), and James Digges La Touche, of Sans Souci, Esqrs., the first Churchwardens. The Rev. Anthony Sillery, A.M. ("distinguished for singleness of mind, genuine piety, unostentatious benevolence, and deep learning," and subsequently well known for his great exertions in behalf of the Waldenses), succeeded Mr. Bulwer in 1825; and during his incumbency, which lasted until 1832 (when he effected an exchange with Mr. Nixon, who held the chaplaincy of Dr. Steevens' Hospital, Dublin), he established the Sunday and Daily Schools, and some of the other existing parochial institutions. The inhabitants are to this day reaping the fruits of his untiring exertions in the cause of God. (*h*)

The parish of Booterstown (termed Ballybotter, Ballyboother, Butterstown, and Boterstone in sundry old documents) comprises the villages of Booterstown and Williamstown, and a small part of the town of Blackrock, with an area of 541 acres (*i*); and forms a very flourishing portion of the large Irish estates of the Right Hon. Sidney Herbert, M.P., who some years since erected and endowed the neighbouring Church of St. John the Evangelist. The district is on the road from Dublin to Kingstown and Bray, and on the southern coast of the bay of Dublin, the shores of which here assume a highly interesting and picturesque appearance. The population, according to the census taken in 1851, amounted to 3,512 (*j*); of whom about 1,800 (the number varying considerably in summer and winter) are members of the United Church of England and Ireland.

PARISH OF DONNYBROOK.

INCUMBENT.
REV. FREDERICK FITZGERALD, A.M.

Donnybrook Parish Church.

This church, dedicated to St. Mary, is a handsome building, in the early style of English architecture, with a vaulted roof and lancet-formed windows. (*k*) It was erected in the year 1827, after a design of John Semple, Esq., at Simmon's-court (likewise known as Symond's-court and Smot's-court) (*l*), close to the river Dodder (*m*), and about midway between the adjacent villages of Donnybrook (in former days termed Dovenachbroc and Donabrok) (*n*) and Ball's-bridge, by means of a loan of £4,153 16s. 11d., from the late Board of First Fruits. The tower was surmounted by a well-proportioned spire, which was so much damaged by the dreadful storm in January, 1839, that it was soon after taken down; and it has not as yet been rebuilt. There is accommodation for about 500 worshippers; the attendance, as in all suburban churches, being larger in the summer than in the winter months.

The old church, situated in the village from which the parish derives its name, and for many years surrounded by a highly respectable and thriving population, was small and inconvenient: the materials of it were sold and removed shortly after the opening of the present church; and of the monuments in the interior, not one was rescued from destruction! (*o*) The graveyard is still in use, and contains the dust of many distinguished individuals, being "rich," according to Archdeacon Cotton, "in buried ecclesiastics." Of the laity we may specify sundry members of the Fitzwilliam family (now represented by the Right Hon. Sidney Herbert); Sir Edward Lovet Pearce, " a celebrated architect, and the builder of the Irish Parliament-house of his day" [ob. 1733] (*p*); Bartholomew Mosse, M.D., founder of the Dublin Lying-in Hospital [ob. 1759] (*q*); and the Rt. Hon. John Radcliff, LL.D., Judge of the Prerogative Court [ob. 1843] (*r*); and of the clergy, Archbishop King [ob. 1729], Bishop Clayton [ob. 1758], and Dean Graves, Regius Professor of Divinity [ob. 1829]. Tombstones, with particulars (which will soon, we hope, be regularly placed on record, in compliance with the notice of the Society of Antiquaries of London), cover the remains of Bishop Clayton and Dean Graves (*s*). Nothing, however, marks the grave of Archbishop King, who, whether we regard him as a prelate, a scholar, or a man of genius, is entitled to a place in the foremost rank of eminent Irishmen; and in the Register of Burials (*t*) merely this concise entry appears:—

"Buried, Archbishop King, May 10th, 1729." (*u*)

Within the limits of the parish, and close to Sandford (*v*), is a truly valuable and interesting institution—the Hospital for Incurables. "The establishment of hospitals for the relief of the poor is, perhaps, one of the most judicious efforts of the human mind. It is to alleviate at once the two most afflicting incidents of human life, and to disarm of their severity the associated evils of poverty and distemper. But there is yet a stage of wretchedness beyond the scope of ordinary hospitals. The unhappy object may be afflicted with a distemper which no medical aid can eradicate, and he then no longer finds an asylum." It is well known that Lord Mornington, father of the late Duke of Wellington (*w*), was the first to interest himself, with effect, for this sorely afflicted class of our fellow-creatures; and that he conceived the happy idea of converting his musical talents into a source of charity, and of appealing to public benevolence through the medium of his favourite science. The Hospital for Incurables was opened in Fleet-street, Dublin, in 1743, and was soon after transferred to Townsend-street, and thence, in 1792, to its present healthful situation. Deriving a very inadequate annual grant from the public funds, it well deserves, and stands much in need of, Christian sympathy and support (x).

Any notice of the parish would certainly be incomplete without a reference to Donnybrook Fair (y). Happily, indeed, through the exertions of some philanthropic individuals the patent has been purchased within the last few years for £3,000, and though there still is a very large concourse of the lower classes at the usual time in the neighbourhood, and a lamentable amount of dissipation, the Fair has been abolished. And was there not good reason for its abolition? Notwithstanding ingenious and unholy attempts, on the part of humourists and ballad-writers, to palliate it by the play of wit and the drollery of fantastic description, "it was for generations a perfect prodigy of moral horrors, a concentration of disgrace upon, not Ireland alone, but civilized Europe." A foreigner, Prince Pückler Muskau, who looked at the saturnalia, said,

"A third part of the public lay, or rather rolled about, drunk; others ate, screamed, shouted, and fought." And a graphic anonymous writer, after instancing the various descriptions of low buffoonery, outrageous indecency, and uproarious rioting, remarks :—" Amidst what is considered by some as mere merriment and mirth, we venture to say there is more misery and madness, devilment and debauchery, than could be found crowded into an equal space of ground in any other part of this our globe, or in any other part of Ireland, during five times the same space which is spent at Donnybrook, in one given year; and, be it remembered, the scenes here described are those which take place during the light of day; the orgies of the night, when every species of dissipation and profligacy is practised without restraint, may be better imagined than described." Thanks to the public authorities, the nuisance had of late years considerably abated ; but, nevertheless, there still remained far more than enough to give the locality an unenviable notoriety over the face of the globe.

The parish of Donnybrook, with an area of 1687 acres, but yielding an inadequate income to the Incumbent, forms a large portion of the corps of the archdeaconry of Dublin, and has lately been constituted a perpetual curacy, the patronage being vested

THE PARISH OF DONNYBROOK. 15

in the Archdeacon. Lying on the south-east side of the city, it embraces the villages of Donnybrook, Clonskeagh, Ball's-bridge, Ringsend, Irishtown, Sandymount, and Merrion. It has a good sprinkling of mansions and villas; and presents, over much of its area, a medium character between town and country (z). The population, according to the census taken in 1851, amounted to 11,178 (aa), of whom the great majority of the upper classes, and a large proportion of the lower, are members of the United Church of England and Ireland.

There are many interesting particulars connected with Sandymount, Merrion, Ringsend, and Irishtown, which we shall reserve for the Sketches of the new Church of St. John the Evangelist, Sandymount, and the old Royal Chapel of St. Matthew, Ringsend.

Sandymount Church.

CHAPLAIN.
REV. WILLIAM DE BURGH, D.D.

THIS church, dedicated to St. John the Evangelist, is in the parish of Donnybrook, close to the seashore, and midway between the villages of Sandymount and Merrion; and is a specimen of the Anglo-Norman style of architecture, which has likewise been designated the Romanesque, the predominance of horizontal lines marking its classical origin. Having been erected and endowed at the sole expense of the Right Hon. Sidney Herbert, to whom almost the entire district belongs, it was opened for Divine service on Sunday, 24th March, 1850, by license from the Archbishop of the diocese, who preached on the occasion, and with whom the nomination to the chaplaincy rested. It was subsequently consecrated by his Grace, the necessary arrangements respecting the grant of the ground not having been completed in the first instance; and standing alone, forms a conspicuous object from the Dublin and Wicklow railway.

In this building, which accommodates about 500, and of which the Rev. William de Burgh, D.D., is the first Chaplain, may be seen many of the distinctive characteristics of the Anglo-Norman style; and as buildings like it are by no means common in Ireland, we think it well to give, in the words of a friend, a brief description of its principal features.

The semicircular arches channelled with chevron and other mouldings—the strong, massive, circular piers or pillars—the doorways deeply recessed, and composed of a succession of receding arches, more or less enriched in the soffits and faces, with different sculptured mouldings—these are distinctive characteristics of the period. The walls are of great thickness, and composed of external facings of cut stone, imported from Caen, the space between being filled with pointed rubble masonry. The narrow, oblong, and semicircular windows are only ornamented externally by a single shaft, and a succession of carved mouldings; and, from the small size of the apertures, and their distance from each other, they impart an appearance of solidity to the structure. The turret, or pinnacle (the summit of which is reached by a winding stone staircase), is placed at the north-west angle, and consists of a cylindrical shaft with a conical capping, pierced by narrow windows. The tower, which is entered from the turret, is short and massive, with a pyramidical stone roof with overhanging eaves, on the four angles of which are sculptured symbolical figures, representing serpents and chimeræ. The buttresses, alternating with the windows, resemble flat pilasters, being a mass of masonry, with a broad surface slightly projecting from the walls. The interior, which is of beautiful workmanship, consists of a nave and side aisles, terminating with a semicircular apse, which forms the chancel, with stained-glass windows. The roof is open, and of wood;

B

and the pulpit, which is placed at the south side of
the nave, below the steps to the chancel, is of Caen
stone, and elaborately carved, the reading-desk
being in the opposite angle. In the nave are eight
plain massive pillars of the same stone, with chisel-
led capitals, supporting the same number of arches,
decorated with chevron, or zig-zag, and other
mouldings; and the seats, which are so arranged as
to form three aisles—a centre and two sides—are
open benches, facing the chancel, and furnished
with stools for kneeling forward. The more objec-
tionable carvings were removed previous to the
consecration of the building, in compliance with the
strongly-expressed opinion of the Archbishop.

Sandymount, according to the "Parliamentary
Gazetteer of Ireland" (1846) "was at one time a
poor place; but it became much improved, acquired
many good houses, and boasted the presence, in
summer, of numerous sea-bathing families from a
distance; yet, while still possessed of much elegance,
and in all respects very superior as a village to its
neighbours—Irishtown, Ringsend, Ball's-bridge, and
Donnybrook—it is far from being unqualifiedly respectable or pleasant." Various improvements have
of late years been effected upon an extensive scale;
and the locality, furnished with many new and large
dwelling-houses, and frequented throughout the year

by a respectable population, is unquestionably a thriving and agreeable suburb.

Merrion, formerly spelt Meryon, or Meryonge (as, for example, in the inscription on the "handsome tomb of black marble" of Oliver Fitzwilliam, Earl of Tyrconnel, which was "in the chapel of the family's foundation in Donnybrooke-Church") (*bb*), is in the south-east quarter of the parish, and almost adjoins Booterstown, a very narrow portion of the parish of Taney (otherwise Tawney, or Tacheny) intervening. Here are several mansions and villas, and the first station of the Dublin and Wicklow railway; and here likewise an old graveyard, in which interments still take place; but when it was consecrated, and by whom, remains a mystery. There is in it, among other tombstones, one of some interest, erected by order of the Earl of Harrington, Commander of the Forces in Ireland, to the memory of a large number of soldiers, chiefly volunteers from the South Mayo Militia into the 18th regiment of the Line, who were lost on the night of the 19th of November, 1807 (when the Prince of Wales packet was wrecked at Dunleary, and the Rochdale transport at Blackrock), and whose bodies, having been washed on the neighbouring shore, were buried in this place (*cc*).

According to the census taken in 1851, the

population of Sandymount (included in the general return of the parish) amounted to 1,419, with an area of 243 acres; and that of Merrion to 725, with an area of 197 acres. The number of inhabitants is now much larger, the majority of them being members of the United Church of England and Ireland.

Irishtown Church.

CHAPLAIN.
REV. RICHARD HENRY WALL, D.D.

This church, properly designated "The Royal Chapel of St. Matthew, Ringsend," but more generally known by the name we have prefixed, is a royal donative chapelry, situated in the parish of Donnybrook, without cure of souls, but subject to episcopal jurisdiction. It was erected in the reign of Queen Anne (but at what cost, and from what funds, is unknown), for the revenue officers and other inhabitants of Ringsend, who were "not only distant from Donabroke, their parish church, but prevented from resorting thither by tides and waters overflowing the highway." Certainly it cannot be commended for architectural beauty, neither outwardly nor inwardly, its most prominent feature being an unsightly square tower; it, however, accommodates about 500 (the Protestant soldiers from Beggarsbush Barracks attending), and is in a quarter where a church is much required; and it is kept in very good repair by the Board of Public Works. The income of the Chaplain and other expenses are defrayed by an annual Parliamentary grant. In November, 1854, the present Chaplain kindly complied with the request of the clergymen of the Parish Church; and, accordingly, Divine service has been conducted by them in both churches every Sunday evening.

Ringsend, according to O'Halloran, was originally called *Rinn-Aun*, signifying "the point of the tide," from its situation by the sea-side, at the confluence of the Dodder with the Liffey (*dd*). Like many other writers, Lord Blayney, in his scarce volume, entitled "Sequel to a Narrative" (1816), has given a very unfavourable report of its condition. "On approaching the town [Dublin] you pass through a vile, filthy, and disgraceful-looking village, called Ringsend. This village [from which a mole, called the South-wall, and 17,754 feet in length, extends to the Pigeon-house and the Light-house (*ee*), and which was for a long period the chief landing and embarking place of Dublin] must make a deep impression on a stranger, certainly giving all the force and all the charm of interest to the grandeur and appearance of the interior of the town." And, according to the " Parliamentary Gazetteer of Ireland " (1846), it is a " dingy, dirty, disagreeable place ; and jointly with Irishtown, forms one of the most befilthified skirts of the city." Nevertheless, as a few facts out of many will suffice to prove, it is a locality of some little note in Irish history. In November, 1646, the Parliamentary forces landed at Ringsend; and in August, 1649, Oliver Cromwell, Lord Lieutenant of Ireland, with a formidable array of men and all the necessaries of war. In 1670, John Lord Berkeley, Baron of Stratton, Lord Lieutenant, landed here. In April, 1690, King James II. (as Story graphically describes the scene in his " Impartial History of the Wars of Ireland," p. 58), visited the village (*ff*). In December, 1691, when De Ginckel was departing for England, the Lords Justices, and most of the nobility and gentry in and about Dublin, accompanied him to Ringsend, where he went on board the Monmouth yacht, and sailed next morning for England. And in 1709, Thomas Earl of Wharton, Lord Lieutenant, landed here. In fact, from an early to a recent date, Ringsend was necessarily visited by almost all who crossed the channel between England and the Irish metropolis; and, therefore, its name frequently appears in connexion with different personages and events. Though it may have been much better in former days (when it was a celebrated bathing resort of the citizens, and afforded, for their accommodation, the public vehicles known as " Ringsend cars ") (*gg*), it was undoubtedly, in our recollection, a very wretched-looking place, and it still is open to serious objection; but, owing to the well-directed plans of its wealthy proprietor, it presents a greatly-improved appearance within the last few years, and promises to become a more respectable and pleasing suburb.

Only a few hundred yards to the south of Ringsend lies the village of Irishtown, in which, as before stated, we find the Royal Chapel of St. Matthew, Ringsend. In the building there are not any monuments of much note (*hh*); while in the graveyard are interred, amongst many others, the Rev. John Borough, first minister of "this royal chapel" [ob. 1726]; Sir James Foulis, Bart., of Colinton, N.B. [ob. 1821]; and Mr. John Macnamara, formerly of Coolnahella, in the county of Clare, and latterly of Sandymount, whose well-known collection of Irish MSS. was dispersed on his death in 1822. A reference to Brooking's curious "Map of the City and Suburbs of Dublin, and also the Archbishop and Earl of Meath's Liberties, with the bounds of each Parish" (1728), will show the great changes that have taken place in the neighbourhood during the last century. Irishtown and its church are represented in the map as almost surrounded by the sea, from which no small extent of ground has been since reclaimed; and the desolate appearance of the country along the south-east side of the bay of Dublin, now so very thickly inhabited, is particularly striking. As a village, Irishtown is superior to Ringsend, and is steadily improving under Mr. Herbert's care; and from its proximity to Dublin and the sea, it is much frequented by strangers during the summer months.

According to the census taken in 1851, the population of Ringsend (included in the general return of the parish) amounted to 2,064, with an area of 54 acres; and that of Irishtown to 1,244, with an area of 57 acres. There are more Protestants of the lower classes (for the most part of English origin) in Ringsend than in any other quarter of the parish.

APPENDIX.

Note (a), p. 7.

CONSECRATION OF BOOTERSTOWN CHURCH.—The following is an extract from the Act of Consecration:—

"We also consecrate the said church to the honor of God and holy uses by the name of the Parish Church of Booterstown, or the Church of Saint Philip and Saint James, Booterstown. And We do pronounce, decree, and declare, that the same hath been, and is, so consecrated, and that it ought so to remain to future times, openly and publickly reserving nevertheless unto Us and our successors, Archbishops of Dublin and Bishops of Glandelagh, a power of visiting the said church when We shall think it our office so to do, in order that We may see whether the same be taken care of in its repairs and ornaments, and whether all things be observed therein canonically and orderly; but as to all the rest of the premises, We, by these presents, do decree and confirm the same, as much as in Us lies, and by law We can, for Us and our successors, Archbishops of Dublin and Bishops of Glandelagh. In testimony whereof We have caused our archiepiscopal seal to be hereunto affixed the sixteenth day of May, in the year of our Lord One Thousand, Eight Hundred, and Twenty-four.

"W. DUBLIN."

The Ven. John Torrens, A.M. (afterwards D.D.), Archdeacon of Dublin, was the preacher.

Note (b), p. 7.

GRANT OF THE SITE.—The following is an extract from the Deed of Conveyance of Ground by the late George Augustus Earl of Pembroke and Montgomery, dated 29th June, 1821 :—

"Provided always that this present grant and conveyance is made upon the express conditions, that a church for the celebration of Divine worship according to the rites and ceremonies of the Established Protestant religion, and to be deemed and considered the chapel or church of the said new parish, district, or cure of Booterstown aforesaid, be erected upon said piece of land with all convenient speed; and also that no part of said ground shall at any time be connected to, or used for the purpose of, a cemetery, or place of burial, within the walls of said church when erected, or without the same; and also that in case it shall happen at any time hereafter that the said piece or parcel of ground, and the buildings thereon erected, shall be used for any other than the purpose hereby declared and intended as aforesaid, then upon any of the said events this present grant and conveyance shall become, and be considered absolutely null and void to all intents and purposes whatsoever."

As already stated, Mr. Herbert has since made a considerable addition to the church-grounds, with a new and handsome approach from Mount Merrion-avenue. A large number of wretched habitations, which were neither an ornament nor a benefit to the neighbourhood, disappeared about the same time from this locality.

Note (c), p. 7.

THE ARCHDEACONRY OF DUBLIN.—For some particulars of the archdeaconry of Dublin, see Monck Mason's "History of St. Patrick's Cathedral, Dublin," p. 44; and Erck's "Irish Ecclesiastical Register" (1830), p. 83. Archdeacon Cotton gives in his "Fasti Ecclesiæ Hibernicæ," Vol. II., pp. 127-132, the succession of the Archdeacons of Dublin, from the year 1180.

Note (d), p. 7.

FORMATION OF BOOTERSTOWN PARISH.—The following is an extract from the Deed:—

"Whereas the Reverend John Torrens, Archdeacon of Dublin, the Curate or Incumbent of said parish of Donnybrook, hath consented by writing or instrument under his hand and seal at the foot of these presents, that the several lands particularly set out and described in the map or survey annexed to these presents, and situate in said parish of Donnybrook, be separated pursuant to said Act from the remaining part of said parish of Donnybrook, and annexed to the aforesaid church of Booterstown, and erected into a new parish, distinct from the said parish of Donnybrook, and which new parish shall be called and known by the name of the Parish of Booterstown, We, the Most Reverend Father in God, John George, by Divine Providence Archbishop of Dublin, Primate and Metropolitan of Ireland, and Bishop of Glandelagh, in whose diocese the said parish lies, have pursuant to the power and authority to Us in this behalf given, with the consent of the said Incumbent, agreed, directed, ordered, consented, and ascertained, and do by these presents agree, declare, direct, order, consent, and ascertain, that the said several lands particularly described and set forth in a map annexed to these presents, that is to say, All That and Those the townlands of Booterstown, situate in the county and diocese of Dublin aforesaid, containing 289A. 2R. 27P. [Irish], be the same more or less (meared and bounded as follows, that is to say, on the north by lands in the possession of Thomas Thorpe Franks, Esq., the representatives of the late Judge Fox, and Mr. Alford; on the east by the sea; on the south partly by the Blackrock, and partly by lands in the possession of the Right Hon. William Saurin, John Verschoyle, and John O'Neill, Esquires; and on the west by the high-road leading from Stillorgan to Dublin), be and are hereby for ever separated, pursuant to said recited Act, from the remaining part of said parish of Donnybrook, and annexed to said church of Booterstown; and We do accordingly erect the same into a new parish or cure, to be called and known by the name of the Parish of Booterstown; and that the said parish of Booterstown is, and shall be, and continue from henceforth, a separate and distinct parish from the said parish of Donnybrook.

And We do constitute, appoint, and declare that the said church and district of Booterstown is, and from henceforth shall be, and continue for ever, a perpetual cure within the meaning of the said Act; and that the curate of said church and his successors, when and as duly nominated and licensed, is, and do, and shall be perpetual curates from henceforth for ever of the said church or new parish, and capable of receiving endowments from all persons and bodies politic and corporate, agreeably to said recited Act and the laws now in being."

It may be well to observe, that by an improvident arrangement of long standing the Incumbent of the adjoining parish of Monkstown receives the tithe rent-charge of Booterstown, though there never has been any connexion between the parishes. Accordingly, when Booterstown was separated from Donnybrook, it was found necessary to provide an income for the new Incumbent from some other source; and with Lord Pembroke's £1,000, and other money in hand, ground-rents in College-street and Fleet-street, Dublin, were purchased in 1821 from the Commissioners of Wide Streets for the sum of £1,333 6s. 8d., in the names of Robert Alexander and James Digges La Touche, Esquires, as detailed in the Deed of Endowment. These rents, amounting to £80 Irish per annum, form (with one or two small additions from other sources) the income of the incumbency of Booterstown.

Note (e), p. 7.

COST OF BUILDING BOOTERSTOWN CHURCH.—Amongst many other documents belonging to the parish, there is one relative to the cost of building the church, &c., with this note by Mr. Sillery:—

" The following document was found amongst the papers left by the late James Digges La Touche respecting the building of the church, and is worth preserving, being the only document which I could find, that conveys an account of the expense attending the building, &c."

Mr. Sillery, in his care of parochial documents, has set a good example to many of his brethren in the ministry.

As stated in the "Fourth Report on Ecclesiastical Revenue and Patronage, Ireland" (1837), p. 19, the cost was "£4,615 7s. 8¼d., British; whereof £3,230 15s. 4¼d. was granted as gift, and £461 10s. 9¼d. as loan, by the late Board of First Fruits, and the residue of £923 1s. 6¼d. was raised by private subscriptions. Of the loan aforesaid, there remained £332 6s. 1d. chargeable on the parish in 1832, repayable by annual instalments of £18 9s. 2d."

Note (f), p. 8.

JAMES DIGGES LA TOUCHE, ESQ.—The following inscription is on his monument:—

"Sacred to the memory of James Digges La Touche, Esq., of Sans Souci, in this parish. 'To him to live was Christ, and to die was gain.' Gifted with great and rare endowments, he dedicated them all to the service of God. In his public life, fervent zeal for the advancement of religion was regulated by the humility of a heavenly wisdom, and consistency of life, with all Christian graces, adorned and illustrated the power of his faith. His was the charity that 'beareth, believeth, hopeth;' while jealousy for the honour of God, and love to the souls of men, made him faithful to admonish. To the Sunday School Society for Ireland, of which he was gratuitous Secretary and Guardian for eighteen years, he devoted much of his heart, his time, his talents; and with holy joy he beheld it spreading its transforming power over this his beloved country. In the domestic circle he was the source, the life, the centre of an elevating and spiritual influence. In early youth he entered the service of a holy Master, and found in that service during his maturer years the felicity of perfect freedom. In the prime of life, aged thirty-eight, his work was done; and when his soul was required by the Lord, he knew the voice of the Good Shepherd, and was 'not afraid.' He entered into glory, Dec. 13th, 1826. 'Blessed are the dead which die in the Lord from henceforth: Yea, saith the Spirit, that they may rest from their labours; and their works do follow them.'"

For particulars of his character, see a "Sermon preached in Booterstown Church, on Sunday, December 17, 1826, noticing the lamented death of James Digges La Touche, Esq.," by the Rev. A. Sillery. (Dublin, 1827.)

RICHARD VERSCHOYLE, ESQ.—The following inscription is on his monument:—

"Sacred to the memory of Richard Verschoyle, of Mount Merrion, who departed this life on the 27th of August, 1827, at Brighton, where, at his own desire, his mortal remains are deposited in a vault in the Parish Church. His unexampled fortitude at the awful moment of being summoned into eternity proved the feelings of a truly religious confidence in the mercy of his Creator. As a sincere and steady friend possessing a mind richly stored with intellectual knowledge, he died universally lamented by an extended circle of acquaintance, and has left a blank in society, as a social and esteemed companion, not easily to be filled up. This tribute of attachment is erected by his afflicted widow in memory of the best of husbands, whose many virtues must ever live in her heart, and who looks forward in the hope of again meeting him in a place of everlasting bliss."

Note (g), p. 8.

THE REV. R. H. NIXON.—"On Thursday morning, the 22nd of January, the Rev. Robert Herbert Nixon entered into rest, in the seventy-fifth year of his age. He has not left his surviving friends without that sense of comfort which springs from a true believer's course on earth; and confident may they be, 'in sure and certain hope of the Resurrection to eternal life through our Lord Jesus Christ,' that he is enjoying the blessed consummation of the prayer so beautifully expressed in Cowper's hymn:—

'Oh! for a closer walk with God,
A calm and heavenly frame;
A light to shine upon the road
That leads me to the Lamb!'

Long will he be remembered in connexion with many a Christian effort. And though he be now removed far beyond the reach of human praise, yet the principle from which these efforts sprang—the spirit of charity, evidenced by these works of love, has passed with him through the grave; and, purified from the alloy of human infirmities, it shall beautify his immortal nature, and shine forth with new splendour in the realms of glory. And (as one who knew him intimately has observed) 'when our minds revert to his Christian character and kindly feelings, be it ours to walk by the same rule—to imitate those features, in which he so strikingly exemplified the mild and attractive graces of the Gospel. Let our wishes for ourselves be moderate, as were his; our motives simple, our kindness unfeigned, our hopes in heaven; let us love as brethren; and the God of love and peace shall be with us. In the flesh we shall see his face no more. But may this separation be succeeded by a joyful welcome in the world of spirits—the welcome of that glorious day when the redeemed shall meet together before the throne of Jesus.' "—From the *Nineteenth Annual Report of the Booterstown and Blackrock Missionary Association.*

In the *Church of England Magazine*, Vol. XLII., p. 207, may be found a sketch of "The Veteran," by an old friend, the Rev. Denis Kelly, Minister of Trinity Church, Goughsquare, London. Mr. Nixon's remains were deposited in a family-vault in Mount Jerome Cemetery.

Note (h), p. 9.

THE REV. ANTHONY SILLERY.—In the *Christian Examiner* (Nos. for December, 1851, and February and July, 1852) there is an interesting biographical sketch of this exemplary servant of God, by one "who knew him the longest and the most intimately," and who thus speaks of his appointment to Booterstown:—

"He had now obtained the great object of his desires—the

cure of souls in the Established Church; and he entered on his duties with earnest and devoted zeal. The circumstances of this parish were such as peculiarly suited his taste. It was in the country, yet so close to the city as to give him all the advantages of a town life. A church had just been erected in it at a cost of nearly £5,000, which for elegance of structure (though small) far surpassed anything of the kind in the viciuity of Dublin. The parish was beautifully situated on the bay of Dublin, and contained numerous villas, where families of distinction resided, amongst whom he could enjoy refined and intellectual society; and it had a large number of poor inhabitants to keep in exercise his active benevolence. Some of the parishioners were men of piety and Christian zeal, ready to unite with him in everything useful. Of these one may be named, the late James Digges La Touche, of Sans Souci, well known for his talents and piety; and whose valuable efforts, especially in the cause of Sunday Schools, won for him universal admiration and esteem. . . . He entered on the duties of this parish with all his heart. He brought its then existing institutions to perfection; he established others. He was loved and respected by the rich, and became the idol of the poor. To this day, though he was there only seven years, and his connexion with it ceased nineteen years ago, the recollection of him is cherished with a freshness of affection truly surprising. His name is pronounced with a blessing by the poor man, and his example appealed to as a pattern for all imitation."

Over his remains in Mount Jerome Cemetery, near the centre of the grounds, is a neat and appropriate tombstone, with the following inscription:—

"Sacred to the memory of the Rev. A. Sillery, who died March 4, 1851, aged sixty-three. He was distinguished for singleness of mind, genuine piety, unostentatious benevolence, and deep learning."

Note (i), p. 9.

BOUNDS OF BOOTERSTOWN PARISH.—Within the bounds of this parish (partly in the barony of Dublin, but chiefly in the half-barony of Rathdown), which are well defined in the Ordnance Survey, the following, with other avenues, are comprised:—Blackrock-road, from Trimleston, Merrion, to Hogan's-lane, Blackrock; George's-avenue (one side); Avoca-avenue (one side); Grove-avenue; Mount Merrion-avenue; Waltham-terrace; Sydney-avenue; Cross-avenue; Southhill-avenue; Stillorgan-road, from Mount Merrion to Seafield; Booterstown-avenue; Gardiner's-row; Williamstown-avenue; and Castledawson-avenue. Carysfort Church, Blackrock (formerly called the Blackstone), is in the parish of Monkstown, only a few yards beyond the bounds of the parish of Booterstown.

Amongst the principal residences are—St. Helen's, of Gen. Lord Viscount Gough; Sans Souci, of Surgeon O'Reilly; Collegnes, of Mrs. D'Olier; Rosemount, of Hugh O'Callaghan, Esq.; Cherbury, of Charles Meara, Esq.; Temora, of Mrs. Purdy; Palermo, of Miss Hudson; Southhill, of James Apjohn, Esq., M.D.; Rokeby, of the Rev. B. H. Blacker; Rockville, of Charles Hopes, Esq.; Marino, of Mrs. Nixon; Glenvar, of John Barrington, Esq.; Beaumont, of Arthur Ormsby, Esq.; Gracefield, of William H. Robinson, Esq.; Avoca Lodge, of George Stormont, Esq.; Frescati, of John Plunkett, Esq.; Deepwell, of Mrs. Guinness; Lisalea, of James W. Macauley, Esq., M.D.; Lisaniskea, of Frederic Willis, Esq.; Pembroke House, of Major Fry; Peafield House, of the Rev. P. N. Kearney; Ruby Lodge, of Thos. Bradley, Esq.; Rosefield, of Edmund M. Kelly, Esq.; Castledawson (vacant); Williamstown Castle, of George Andrews, Esq.; Willow Park, of Henry Bewley, Esq.; Chesterfield (vacant); Bellevue, of Edward Browne, Esq.; Lota, of Lady O'Donel; Clareville, of John Bolton Massey, Esq.; and Dawson Court, of William O'Connor Morris, Esq.

There is amongst the parish documents a "transcript of map and survey made by Messrs. Sherrard, Brassington, and Green, 1820, and attached to the Deed for erecting the townland of Booterstown into a parish of ease to St Mary's, Donnybrook, which was comprised of the townlands of Sim-

c

monscourt, 110A., Moyerry, 80A., and Booterstown, 240A. (total 430A.), old admeasurement. Taken from an ancient record in Headford Library, Trim." But the parish of Donnybrook was then, and is now, even with the loss of Booterstown, of wider extent than would appear from the foregoing statement.

By Act of 5 and 6 Vict. c. 96, the townland of Intake, in this parish, has been transferred from the ancient county of the city to the new barony of Dublin.

The exact area of the parish is as follows:—471A. 0R. 13P. in the half-barony of Rathdown; and 70A. 0R. 35P. in the barony of Dublin; total, 541A. 1R. 8P.

Note (j), p. 9.

POPULATION OF BOOTERSTOWN PARISH. — The Act of 55 Geo. III. afforded the first opportunity of ascertaining the population of Ireland by the actual enumeration of its inhabitants, carried on under the sanction of the Legislature; and consequently the census taken in the year 1821 is the first authentic statement of the actual number of souls in Ireland. In this year, however, no separate return was made for the parish of Booterstown, the numbers being included in the return for Donnybrook. "The number of houses and souls in the village of Williamstown is not specified; but Booterstown is returned as containing 158 houses."

In 1831, when the next census was taken, the population amounted to 3,549; comprising 1,454 males and 2,095 females; forming 595 families; and occupying 451 houses. There were also 46 houses uninhabited or building.

In 1841, the population amounted to 3,318; comprising 1,312 males and 2,006 females; forming 639 families; and occupying 518 houses. There were also 47 houses uninhabited or building.

In 1851, as stated in the text, the population amounted to 3,512; comprising 1,336 males and 2,176 females; forming 701 families; and occupying 570 houses. There were also 60 houses uninhabited or building.

The foregoing particulars have been carefully gleaned from the different Census Reports; and those who wish to have full and satisfactory information are strongly recommended to consult the same authorities, and not to give way to the ignorant prejudice too commonly entertained against all Parliamentary blue-books. The last Report in particular (complete in six parts, or ten volumes, 1852–56) contains a vast amount of useful and interesting information respecting Ireland from a very early period to the year 1851.

Note (k), p. 10.

DONNYBROOK CHURCH.—A woodcut of this building, which is frequently called Simmonscourt Church, is given in the *Dublin Penny Journal*, Vol. I., p. 212. It is there represented with its slender spire, as before the great storm in 1839, and without any enclosure. The writer has likewise in his possession two well-executed drawings by a Dublin artist; and differing in some respects, they give a fair idea of what the building was, and what it is.

The cost of building, as stated in the text, and in the "Fourth Report on Ecclesiastical Revenue and Patronage, Ireland" (1837), p. 87, was "£4,153 16s. 11d., British, granted [in November, 1825] in way of loan by the late Board of First Fruits; of which loan there remained £3,825 3s. chargeable on the parish in 1832, repayable by annual instalments of £166 3s."

Note (l), p. 10.

SYMOND'S-COURT TOWER.—A view of Symond's-court Tower, drawn by T. Cocking in 1790, may be found in Grose's "Antiquities of Ireland," Vol. I., p. 21, with a short account. This ancient structure was probably built to secure the surrounding property of the Dean and Chapter of Christ Church from the rapacity of the Wicklow mountaineers, and is situated within the grounds of B. M. Tabuteau, Esq.

Note (m), p. 10.

THE DODDER.—"*Dothair* (fem.) *Dothra*. This is the ancient Irish form of the name of the river Dodder, in the county of Dublin. The church of Achadh Finiche is described in the *Feilire Ænguis*, at 11th of May, and in the Irish calendar of the O'Clerys, as on the brink of the Dothair, in the territory of Ui Dunchadha, in Leinster."—" The Book of Rights," edited by Mr. O'Donovan for the Celtic Society, p. 12, n.

Note (n), p. 10.

DONNYBROOK.—In "Registrum Prioratus Omnium Sanctorum juxta Dublin," edited by Dean Butler for the Irish Archæological Society, frequent mention is made of Donnybrook. Of the documents in the Registry, No. I., " Confirmacio Gregorii [IX.] spiritualium et temporalium cum certis privilegiis et aliis immunitatibus," A.D. 1234, speaks of "quadraginta acras sitas in territorio de Donenachbroc [recte Dovenachbroc] versus aquilonem;" No. LXXV., " De Donabroke," ante 1234; No. LXXVI., " De trigenta novem acris apud Donabrok," ante 1234; No. LXXVII., "De eadem terra," A.D. 1298; and No. LXXVIII., " De aqua de Dodyr ducenda," &c., A.D. 1307. No. I. in the Appendix, from the archives of the city of Dublin, is " De tenemento de Donenachbrok." Very absurd is the derivation of the name given by Mr. and Mrs. S. C. Hall, in their " Ireland; its Scenery, Character," &c., Vol. II., p. 338:—"'Donnybrook'—the little brook—is so called from a mountain stream, ' the Dodder,' which runs through the suburb."

Note (o), p. 11.

THE OLD CHURCH OF DONNYBROOK.—" Considerable attention being now directed towards the preservation of monumental inscriptions, I am induced to put the following Query, in the hope of an answer from some one of your Irish correspondents. What became of the materials of the old parish church of Donnybrook? They were very improperly sold, I believe, about thirty years ago, shortly after the opening of the present parish church, and probably were soon beyond recovery. As there were several monuments in the interior of the building, not one of which was transferred to the new building, or (as far as I am aware) left behind by the purchaser in the graveyard, it is desirable to ascertain, if possible, whether they are still in existence. . . . The large iron gates, I may add, serve to ornament and protect a neighbouring fruit-garden: but the fate of the monuments has so far baffled my inquiries." (*Notes and Queries*, 2nd S., vi. 147.) A small portion of one of the walls is standing; and the old baptismal font is preserved in the present building. Mr. D'Alton, in his "History of the County of Dublin," p. 801, enumerates several, besides those mentioned in the text, who have been interred in the churchyard, and whose tombstones may be found. Accurate copies of many of the inscriptions, for which there is not room here, are in the writer's possession. For a reference to sundry improvements effected in this yard a few years since, see *Saunders's News-Letter*, 12th March, 1847; or the *Irish Ecclesiastical Journal*, vol. iv. p. 246.

Note (p), p. 11.

SIR EDWARD LOVET PEARCE.—Sir Edward L. Pearce, M.P. for Ratoath, died in his house at Stillorgan (otherwise Stacklorgan), in the county of Dublin, in the year 1733, and was interred at Donnybrook, where, however, no memorial of him can be discovered. There also was subsequently interred his brother, Lieutenant-General Thomas Pearce, who had displayed great courage and abilities in Spain and Portugal, and who, besides being a Privy Councillor, was at once Governor, Mayor, and Representative in Parliament of the city of Limerick.—Ferrar's " History of Limerick," p. 83.

Note (q), p. 11.

BARTHOLOMEW MOSSE, M.D.—" Several physicians attended him, but, finding all their endeavours ineffectual, they advised him to return into the country. On this occasion Alderman Peter Barrè made him the kind offer of his house at Cullenswood (about a mile from town), which the Doctor readily accepted; and there, on the 16th of February following [1759], he departed this life in the forty-seventh year of his age, and was interred at Donnybrook, leaving the new hospital a monument to posterity of his surprising perseverance, diligence, and ingenuity, and indeed one of the most superb architectural ornaments of the great and elegant city of Dublin." See a " Biographical Memoir of Bartholomew Mosse, M.D." (Dublin, 1846.) " We," his biographer adds, " have made diligent but unsuccessful search for the tomb of Mosse at Donnybrook."

Note (r), p. 11.

THE RIGHT HON. JOHN RADCLIFF, LL.D.—The following inscription is on his tombstone:—

" Here are interred the mortal remains of the Right Hon. John Radcliff, LL.D., who died on the 18th July, 1843, in the 78th year of his age. For 27 years he fulfilled the offices of Judge of the Prerogative Court and Vicar-General of Dublin; during which period he devoted himself with unexampled diligence to the publick service, combining abilities of the highest order with untiring patience and spotless integrity. In him is lost to his family and friends a sincere Christian, gifted with the sweetest temper and most affectionate heart; and to the poor a sure benefactor. 'Mark the perfect man, and behold the upright; for the end of that man is peace.'—Psalm xxxvii. 87."

Dr. Radcliff had been likewise for many years Vicar-General of Armagh, in which office he was succeeded by the late Rev. George Miller, D.D., author of "Modern History Philosophically Illustrated," and of many other publications, and whose judgments on points of ecclesiastical law are highly esteemed.

Note (s), p. 12.

BISHOP CLAYTON.—The following inscription is still legible on a very large stone:—

"Here lyeth ye body of Doctor Robert Clayton, Lord Bishop of Clogher, who was born in the year 1695, and was elected Fellow of Trinity College in 1714. He resigned his Fellowship in the year 1728; and the same year married Katherine, daughter of Lord Chief Baron Donnellan. He was promoted to the Bishoprick of Killala in the year 1729, and died in 1758, in the 64th year of his age. To enumerate all his amiable qualities would take up too much room for this place. His character as a Christian, and abilities as a writer, appear by his works. He lived esteemed by good men; he died regretted by many, most lamented by his afflicted widow."

He was co-opted to a Senior Fellowship in 1724, which he resigned on his marriage. In 1733, he was translated from the see of Killala to that of Cork and Ross, and thence to Clogher in 1745. "A censure [for his peculiar opinions] was certain: a deprivation was apprehended. But, before the time appointed arrived, he was seized with a nervous fever, which brought him to his dissolution [at his house in St. Stephen's-green] on the 26th of February, 1758."— Bishop Mant's "History of the Church of Ireland," Vol. II., pp. 613–618.

RICHARD GRAVES, D.D., DEAN OF ARDAGH.—"In the detailed and interesting Memoir prefixed to 'The Works of Richard Graves, D.D., Dean of Ardagh, and Regius Professor of Divinity in the University of Dublin' (4 vols. 8vo.)

the date of his death is given; but no mention is made of the place of his interment. It may be well, for more reasons than one, to record the locality in *Notes and Queries;* and therefore I am induced to send a copy of an entry in the register of burials in the parish of Donnybrook. The following is No. 157 :—

" ' The Very Reverend Richard Graves, of Harcourt-street, in the parish of St. Peter [Dublin], aged sixty-five, was buried this 3rd day of April, 1829.'

" A stone, with an inscription, covers the grave of this learned divine and servant of God, in the old churchyard of Donnybrook."—*Notes and Queries,* 1st S., x. 203.

The following is the inscription on the tombstone (much broken) over the family-vault :—

" Here are deposited the remains of Matilda Jane, wife of Robert James Graves, Esq., M.D., who died Sept. the 1st, 1825, aged 19 years.

" Elizabeth Mary, wife of the Rev. Dr. Graves, Dean of Ardagh, who died March 22, 1827, aged 60 years.

" And Sarah, second wife of Robert James Graves, who died June the 16th, 1827, aged 26 years.

" And of the Very Rev. Richard Graves, D.D., Dean of Ardagh, who died March 31, 1829, aged 65 years.

" And of Eliza Drew Jane F. Graves, second and only surviving daughter of Robt. James Graves and Matilda Jane his first wife, who died on the 4th March, 1831, aged 5 years and 6 months.

" And of John Graves, Esq., nephew to the above Richard Graves, D.D., died the 13th January, 1835, aged 58 years."

The only monument in Donnybrook Church has this inscription :—

" In affectionate remembrance of John Crosbie Graves, Esq., Barrister-at-law, second son of the Very Rev. Thomas Graves, Dean of Connor, this tablet was erected by his afflicted widow. The upright and efficient discharge of his public duties as a Magistrate of Police, and Commissioner of Bankrupts, won for him the esteem of his fellow-citizens;

and the union of refined tastes with warm and delicate feelings peculiarly endeared him to his private friends. His family, upon whose hearts is engraven the memory of his unwearied kindness and humble piety, can never cease to deplore his loss. He died in Dublin, Jan. 13, 1835, aged 58 years, and is buried in the old churchyard of this parish, in the family-vault of his uncle, the Very Rev. Richard Graves, D.D., Dean of Ardagh."

Note (t), p. 12.

DONNYBROOK PARISH REGISTERS.—" In the hope that it may lead to their recovery, if still in existence, I wish to state in *Notes and Queries*, that among the records belonging to the parish of Donnybrook, near Dublin, there is not the vestige of a register of baptisms, marriages, or burials (and there must have been many of these occurrences in so large a parish), for the space of thirty-two years before 1800. How the book or books were lost, or when, no one can tell; but certain I am that they have not been forthcoming, to the great inconvenience and injury of many persons, for the last fourteen years. The registers of the parish date from 1712." (*Notes and Queries*, 2nd S., vii. 217.) A few entries of baptisms, &c., from 9th August, 1705, to the year 1712, and also seventeen marriages by the Rev. Gore Wood, 1778-84, are inserted in the oldest book extant; and it is to be presumed that registers of an earlier date existed, though for many years past they have not been forthcoming. For some remarks on Parish Registers, see "Postulates and Data," pp. 194-205 (London, 1852.)

Note (u), p. 12.

ARCHBISHOPS KING AND MAGEE.—"Archbishop King died May 8, 1729, and was buried in the churchyard of Donnybrook [on the north side, as he had directed in his lifetime]; but no monument or other memorial of him can now be found there. Archbishop Magee died August 19, 1831, and was buried in the old churchyard of Rathfarnham, likewise not far from Dublin. His tomb stands exactly in the centre of the ancient church; but as no inscription has been placed on it, the spot will ere long be forgotten. This treatment appears somewhat strange in connexion with two of the ablest and greatest of the archbishops of Dublin. It ought, one would think, to be corrected; and yet perhaps Sir William Jones' plan is the wisest: 'The best monument that can be erected to a man of literary talents is a good edition of his works.'"—*Notes and Queries*, 2nd S., i. 148.

Note (v), p. 12.

SANDFORD.—Mention of this place naturally recals to one's mind the late Ven. Henry Irwin, of whom it has been well observed by his successor in the chaplaincy, the Rev. W. P. Walsh, in the Notice prefixed to his "Remains," p. xxv., that "it was in his beloved church and parsonage, at Sandford, that Archdeacon Irwin gathered around him the deep love of that inner circle of friends and hearers who were there privileged to attend upon his faithful teaching. By a ministry of two-and-thirty years he made that quiet spot a consecrated ground, and hallowed it into a centre from which blessed influences were diffused upon the Church and country that he loved." Sandford Church is in the parish of St. Peter, Dublin, only a few yards beyond the bounds of the parish of Donnybrook.

Note (w), p. 12.

THE DUKE OF WELLINGTON.—"It was not in India, as commonly supposed, but on Donnybrook-road, that his first laurels were won. This appears from the *Freeman's Journal*, September 18th, 1789, where we learn that in consequence of a wager between him and Mr. Whaley of one hundred and fifty guineas, the Hon. Arthur Wesley walked from the five-mile-stone on Donnybrook-road to the corner of the Circular-road in Leeson-street, in fifty-five minutes, and that a number of gentlemen rode with the walker, whose horses he kept in a tolerable smart trot. When it is recollected that those were Irish miles, even deducting the distance from Leeson-street to the Castle, whence the original measurements were made, this walk must be computed at nearly six English miles."—*Notes and Queries,* 1st S., viii. 491.

Note (x) p. 13.

THE HOSPITAL FOR INCURABLES. — The Buckingham Hospital, near the Donnybrook-road, originally intended for a small-pox hospital, was, for some time prior to 1792, used as a Lock hospital; but being insufficient for the purpose, and inconveniently situated for the necessary medical attendance, it was in that year transferred to the governors of the charitable foundation for incurables, who gave in exchange their hospital in Townsend-street, which has since that time been denominated the Westmoreland Lock Hospital, from the nobleman who was then Viceroy, and at whose instance the exchange was effected.

The following extracts are from a recent appeal to the citizens of Dublin from the Governors of the Hospital for Incurables:—

"The Hospital is situated near Donnybrook, in a peculiarly healthful and secluded situation; and although so pre-eminently an institution of mercy, and altogether peculiar, both in the objects that it relieves, and the relief that it affords, is too little known, and has consequently not met with as large a portion of public sympathy as it so well merits.

"The Institution is intended for those whom incurable disease has rendered incapable of effort; it therefore does not aim beyond the alleviation of confirmed and hopeless disease. The victims of Cancer, Consumption, Paralysis, and of every variety of incurable malady, are received within its walls, and are nursed with unremitting care and tenderness. It receives those who are rejected as incurable from other sanatory institutions, and is the last refuge on this side the grave for suffering mortality combined with poverty.

"This account is in no respect exaggerated, and every person who will walk through its wards may satisfy himself of the truth of this statement. He will there witness permanent, unmixed suffering—disgusting and wasting disease—and a wretched, hopeless struggle with pain and debility. All that can be effected by medical care, by judicious nourishment (which in many instances is necessarily costly), and by tender watchfulness, is freely given; and the Governors have the satisfaction of stating, that the Hospital has in every case been a blessing, and an acknowledged blessing, to its incurable inmates."

For many interesting particulars connected with the Hospital (including a copy of the charter of incorporation granted by King George III., 7th January, 1800), see the "Report of the Commissioners appointed to inspect Charitable Institutions, Dublin" (1842), pp. 118–135; the "Report of the Commissioners appointed to inquire into the Hospitals of Dublin" (1855); and the "First and Second Annual Reports of the Board of Superintendence of Dublin Hospitals" (1858 and 1859).

Note (y), p. 13.

DONNYBROOK FAIR.—In the year 1204 King John granted his license to the corporation of Dublin to hold an eight-day fair at Donnybrook, commencing on the day of the finding of the Holy Cross (3rd May), with similar stallages and tolls as established in Waterford and Limerick. King Henry III., by charter in 1252, extended the duration of the Fair to fifteen days, and changed the day of its commencement to the 7th of July; which was further altered to the 10th of the same month, and by a subsequent charter fixed to the 26th of August. Many attempts have been made from time to time to curtail the nuisance, with more or less success; and the patent passed through various hands until it reached the representatives of the late John Madden, Esq., of Donnybrook, from whom it was purchased, in 1855, for the sum of £3,000.

Since the foregoing paragraph was in type, a copy of the following " Statement in relation to the Fair of Donnybrook " (through the kindness of R. R. Madden, Esq., M.D.) has been furnished by Thomas Carmichael, Esq., who was professionally engaged in the purchase of the patent; and being an important document, it is inserted in full, though, when compared with what immediately precedes it, a few repetitions and slight differences cannot fail to be seen:—

"By a King's Letter enrolled in the Close Roll of the sixth year of King John (1204) in the Tower of London, that King commanded Meiler FitzHenry, Justiciary of Ireland, amongst other things, 'as he had informed the King that he had not a place where the King's treasure could be safely deposited, and that for this cause and many other necessary causes a fortress was required,' to build a castle in a proper place, and to protect and defend the city, and to surround it with a fosse and walls fortified with competent towers, bulwarks, and other defences, as he should consider the King's peace and safety; and that for this purpose he should get 300 marks, owing by E. FitzRobert. He commanded also by letters patent that his citizens of Dublin should have the city enclosed, and that they should be compelled to do so, if unwilling.

"He willed also that there should be a fair at Donnybrook every year for eight days' duration, at the Invention of the Holy Cross (3rd May), and another at the well of St. John the Baptist, likewise for eight days, allowing to them toll and stallage; another at Waterford, on the day of St. Peter in Chains; another at Limerick, on the feast of St. Martin, for eight days; and he commanded these things to be announced, that all merchants should come there freely. Witnessed, &c., 31st day of August. (The original record of Chancery, and the translation, preserved in the Tower of London.)

"The right of the citizens to hold this fair is recognised in two other letters of the same King, also enrolled in the Close Roll of the sixteenth and seventeenth years of his reign (1214 and 1215); and by the latter, the time for holding the fair is enlarged to fifteen days, saving to the Archbishop of Dublin the said fair for the first two days thereof.

"By charter dated 1241, 26th Henry III., reciting that he had granted, and by that his charter confirmed, to his citizens of Dublin that they and their heirs for ever should have a fair at Dublin within their bounds every year for fifteen days, that is to say, on the vigil, the day, and the morrow of the Translation of St. Thomas the Martyr, and for twelve days following, which they had theretofore had, by grant of King John his father, beginning at the feast of the Invention of the Holy Cross for fifteen days, saving to the Archbishop of Dublin and his successors the aforesaid fair for two days, that is to say, the vigil of the said Translation and the day of the same; therefore the King willed and firmly commanded for him, his heirs, and successors for ever, that his said citizens of Dublin and their heirs for ever should have a fair for ever within their bounds every year for fifteen days' duration, that is to say, on the vigil, the day, and the morrow of the Translation of St. Thomas the Martyr, and for twelve days following, with all liberties and free customs to the same fair belonging, which they had hitherto held by grant of the Lord John the King, his father, commencing on the vigil of the Invention of the Holy Cross, for fifteen days' duration, saving to the Venerable Father Lord Archbishop of Dublin and his successors, of the said fair two days, that is to say, the vigil and the day of the Translation aforesaid. Witnesses, W. Bishop of Worcester; Richard le Clare, Earl of Gloucester and Hertford; Master William de Kilkenny, Archdeacon of Coventry. Given under the King's hand, 28th May.

"By charter dated 1279, 8th Edward I., the time of commencing the fair was further postponed at the instance of the citizens, and for their greater convenience, as therein stated, to the eve of the Translation of St. Benedict the Abbot, in July, to be held for fifteen days.

"By a subsequent charter the time of holding the fair was changed to a still later period; and from time immemorial the same has been held in the Green of Donnybrook, on the 26th of August, continuing during periods varying from a week to fifteen days.

"Although some title on the part of the Archbishop of

Dublin to two out of the fifteen days during which the fair was to last, is alluded to in some of the late charters, there is no trace on record of its ever being exercised.

"The corporation of the city of Dublin having in the course of time absolutely disposed of the right of holding this fair, with the tolls and customs thereof under the aforesaid charters, the same, upon the death of Henry Ussher (the preceding proprietor) in the year 1756, became vested in Sir William Wolseley, Bart., who in the year 1778 made a lease thereof to the late Joseph Madden, of Donnybrook; and in the year 1812 the then Baronet absolutely assigned same for ever to the late John Madden, his [Joseph Madden's] son, by the representatives of whom, and of Peter Madden his brother, the same were conveyed in the year 1855 to the Right Hon. Joseph Boyce, then Lord Mayor of the city of Dublin, and Edward Wright, Esq., LL.D., in trust for the Committee then formed for the abolition of said Donnybrook Fair, and for their fellow-citizens subscribing to the contribution."

The following extracts are from the circular issued by the Committee for the Abolition of Donnybrook Fair:—

"The annals of social and commercial life in this metropolis afford sad and abundant records of the ruin and degradation which, dating their commencement with a visit to this Fair, have befallen many who once enjoyed a character for industry and morality, and who, but for the contamination there contracted, might still have enjoyed it.

"The facts, that large sums of money are annually drawn from the Savings' Banks, to be squandered at the Fair; that every anniversary is followed by a fearful increase of disease, as attested by the Hospital and Dispensary Reports; and that the amount of crime, as shown by the Police Reports, is fearfully augmented, afford conclusive evidence as to the vast amount of social mischief generated on these occasions.

"Deluded by the specious show of recreation and amusement, multitudes are caught in the meshes of temptation, and allured into the snares of vice. Servants, mechanics, tradesmen, and even clerks and shopmen, all in respectable employment, have been thus led into courses which have entailed the loss of situation, the forfeiture of character, and consequent misery to themselves and their families. To the young of both sexes it has been the source of unnumbered evils, whilst, to young females especially, it has proved an easy and fatal descent into the lowest depths of infamy and shame.

"Happily, an opportunity for putting an end to the occasion of these evils now presents itself. The proprietors of the patent under which the Fair is held, are willing to surrender their claims for £3,000; a sum which, if considered in relation to their vested interests, is fair and reasonable, and if compared with the amount of good to be accomplished, is trifling and insignificant.

"The Committee invite the aid and co-operation of every friend of religion and morality, to the completion of a work now auspiciously begun."

Though the patent was purchased, and safely vested in the hands of those who will not abuse it, the expectations of the Committee and Subscribers were not at once realised. An individual, who lives in Donnybrook, and has had for some time past the lease and license of a public-house, with a field attached to her holding, persisted in having a fair on her premises, and occasioned no small amount of damage to the public; but THE FAIR has been abolished, and it is to be hoped that ere long no traces of it may be found. For a strong, but not too strong article on the subject, see the *Irish Times*, 23rd August, 1859.

It is satisfactory to be able to add, that cogent reasons against the renewal of the license having been urged by the Crown, and both sides of the case fully argued, in the College-street Police Office, the presiding Magistrates have given judgment against Miss Eliza Dillon, as detailed in *Saunders's News-Letter*, 9th November. The certificate for her license has been very properly refused; and thus the so-called fair of Donnybrook is at an end.

Note (z), p. 15.

BOUNDS OF DONNYBROOK PARISH.—Within the bounds of this parish (partly in the half-barony of Rathdown and

NOTES. 49

barony of Uppercross, but chiefly in the barony of Dublin), which are well defined in the Ordnance Survey, the following, with other avenues, are comprised :—Donnybrook-road, from Upper Leeson-street to Donnybrook; Stillorgan-road, from Donnybrook to Priesthouse; Clonskea-road, from Cullenswood-terrace to Clonskea; Sallymount; Bushfield-avenue; Belmont-avenue; Seaview-terrace; Simmonscourt; Blackrock-road, from the College Botanic Gardens to Trimleston, Merrion; Beggarsbush-road; Bath-avenue, with Vavasour-square; Sandymount-road, from near Ringsend-bridge to Sandymount; Irishtown-strand; London-bridge-road; Tritonville-avenue; Serpentine-avenue; Sandymount-avenue; Sandymount-green; Seafort-avenue; Newgrove-avenue; Sandymount-strand; Park-avenue; Sydney-parade; Merrion-strand; White's-avenue; and Merrionview-avenue.

Amongst the principal residences are—Nutley, of Alderman Roe, D.L.; Woodview, of Captain Frederick J. Isacke; Greenfield, of Randle H. M'Donnell, Esq.; Thornfield, of Richard Wilson, Esq.; Montrose, of Wm. Jameson, Esq.; Airfield, of James Jameson, Esq.; Mount Errol, of William Bredin, Esq.; Shamrock-hill, of Edward Hornsby, Esq.; Plantation, of John Hewson, Esq.; Floraville, of Edward Wright, Esq., LL.D.; Vergemount, of Patrick Donegan, Esq.; Swanbrook, of the Rev. John L. Chute; St. Ann's, of Colonel O'Neill; Simmonscourt Castle, of Bartholomew M. Tabuteau, Esq.; Erith Lodge, of John Spain, Esq.; Willfield, of Mrs. Clarke; Willfield House, of Miss O'Reilly; Sandymount Castle, of Robert Corbet, Esq.; Claremont, of Mrs. Lovely; Belvedere, of the Hon. Mrs. Butler; Fairfield House, of Thomas Reilly, Esq.; Kirkville, of Alex. Sanson, Esq.; Elm Park, of Joseph Watkins, Esq.; Lowville, of Robert Murray, Esq.; Bloomfield, of Mrs. Aylmer; and Merrion Castle, of Mrs. Low.

Amongst the maps of the Down (*i.e.*, "laid down") Survey, safely deposited in the Custom-house, Dublin, there is one of " the Parishes of Donnabrook and Tannee [Taney], somewhat

D

worn at the edges." See the "Supplement to the Third Report of the Irish Record Commissioners" (1813); and also Sir William Petty's "History of the Down Survey" (1655–6), edited by the present Major-General Larcom for the Irish Archæological Society.

In Hardiman's "Catalogue of Maps, Charts, and Plans relating to Ireland, preserved amongst the MSS. in Trinity College, Dublin" (1824), p. 10, there is mention of "a manuscript plan of an encampment, without name or date. It appears, however, to have been in the neighbourhood of Dublin, from the outlet marks, as follow:—St. Steven's-street waye; Colledge-green waye; Baggatrough-waye; Dunnabroke-waye; St. Kevan's-street waye; and may have reference to the situation of the Marquis of Ormond's camp before the fatal battle with Colonel Michael Jones, near Dublin, in 1649."

By Act of 5 and 6 Vict. c. 96., the townlands of Bagotrath, Ballsbridge, Beggarsbush, Clonskeagh (formerly Clanskiagh) Donnybrooke east and west, Forty-acres, Irishtown, Merrion, Ringsend, Sandymount, and Smotscourt, in this parish, have been transferred from the ancient county of the city to the new barony of Dublin.

The exact area of the parish is as follows:—1313A. 2R. 9P. in the barony of Dublin; 363A. 3R. 26P. in the half-barony of Rathdown; and 10A. 2R. in the barony of Uppercross; total, 1687A. 3R. 35P. *

Note (aa), p. 15.

POPULATION OF DONNYBROOK PARISH.—According to the census taken in the year 1821, which (as already mentioned) is the first authentic statement of the actual number of souls in Ireland, the population of the parish of Donnybrook, including Booterstown, amounted to 9,219; comprising 4,267 males and 4,952 females; forming 2,049 families; and occupying 1,235 houses. There were also 96 houses uninhabited or building.

In 1831, when the next census was taken, the population amounted to 10,394; comprising 4,729 males and 5,665 females; forming 2,170 families; and occupying 1,212 houses. There were also 100 houses uninhabited or building.

In 1841 the population amounted to 9,825; comprising 4,464 males and 5,361 females; forming 1,865 families; and occupying 1,244 houses. There were also 106 houses uninhabited or building.

In 1851, as stated in the text, the population amounted to 11,178; comprising 4,971 males and 6,207 females; forming 2,229 families; and occupying 1,524 houses. There were also 175 houses uninhabited or building.

[For some particulars not here repeated, see Note (*j*), p. 84.]

Note (bb), p. 19.

OLIVER EARL OF TYRCONNEL.—" In Archdall's edition of ' Lodge's Peerage of Ireland,' Vol. IV., p. 318, it is stated that the Earl of Tyrconnel lies buried under a handsome tomb of black marble, in the chapel of the family's foundation in Donnybrooke-Church, with this inscription, over which are the arms of Fitzwilliam, and the coronet, but no crest or supporters :—

" 'Here lyeth the Body of the Right Honourable and most Noble Lord Oliver, Earl of Tyrconnel, Lord Viscount Fitzwilliams of Meryonge, Baron of Thorn-Castle, who died at his House in Meryong April 11th, 1667, and was Buried the 12th day of the same month.'

" As I can testify from my own observation, the church, chapel, and this and many other tombs (Archbishop King's included [if he had one]) have disappeared ; but when and how, I cannot tell."—*Notes and Queries*, 2nd S., iv. 90.

Note (cc), p. 19.

TOMBSTONE IN MERRION GRAVEYARD. — The following inscription is on the tombstone:—

" Sacred to the memory of the soldiers belonging to his Majesty's 18th Regiment of Foot, and a few belonging to other corps, who, actuated by a desire of more extensive service, nobly volunteered from the South Mayo and different regiments of Irish Militia into the Line, and who were unfortunately shipwrecked on this coast in the Prince of Wales packet, and perished on the night of the 19th of November, 1807. This tribute to their memory has been placed on their tomb by order of General the Earl of Harrington, Commander of the Forces in Ireland."

In the old churchyard of Carrickbrennan, in the parish of Monkstown, there is a stone in memory of Major Charles Gormocan, who perished in the Rochdale transport; and near the entrance is a mound thrown over, and a stone commemorative of the unfortunate officers and soldiers of the 97th regiment.

THE "PRINCE OF WALES" AND THE "ROCHDALE."— The Rev. C. H. Minchin has supplied these particulars from an old scrap among his *disjecta membra variorum* :—

"Dublin, 19th November, 1807.—On Wednesday morning the 'Prince of Wales,' Captain Edwards, sailed from our port for Liverpool, in company with two transports. They were perceived working about the bay on Thursday morning; and when the fall of snow commenced, it was supposed they were endeavouring to regain the harbour. The snow fell so thickly, that they were not able to discern their way; and the surge, even if they did, broke so violently against the beach, that they could not come to an anchor. The 'Prince of Wales' struck immediately under the battery of Dunleary point, when Captain Edwards, the crew, and two officers immediately hoisted out the boat, jumped into it, and gained the shore. The remainder of the passengers, 120 in number, volunteers from the South Mayo regiment for the 97th and 18th, unfortunately perished in the wreck. The point at which she struck is immediately opposite Sir John Lees' house, Seapoint. The transports which sailed in company with the 'Prince of Wales' have not yet been heard of. Among those lost in the 'Prince of Wales' was Lieutenant Maclean, a promising young man, who had the care of the recruits.

"The 'Rochdale' of Liverpool sailed on the same day, in company with seven transports, for England. On Thursday she was discovered in the offing off Blackrock, in great distress. The blue lights were hoisted, and the guns repeatedly fired. The state of the weather and the violence of the surge prevented any succour from reaching them. She had on board part of the 97th, or Queen's Germans; and some volunteers from the South Cork and Mayo regiments were also on board. The embarkation-return of this vessel is as follows:—1 major, 2 lieutenants, 1 ensign, 8 serjeants, 9 corporals, 173 rank and file, 42 women, and 29 children; in all 265 souls, not one individual of whom is known to have escaped. The names of the officers were—Major Gormocan, 97th Foot; Lieutenants Long and Power, and Ensign Way. The vessel lies alongside of the Tower. Her bottom is completely bilged, though her decks are said to remain entire. A great part of the beach from Dunleary to the Rock was covered with the dead bodies, &c."

Note (dd), p. 21.

DERIVATION OF "RINGSEND."—According to a writer in *Notes and Queries*, 2nd S., ii. 315, " the explanation of this apparent bull, *ring's end*, is very simple. Previous to the formation of that portion of Dublin which is now called Sir John Rogerson's-quay, there were great piles of wood driven into the sand, and to each of these piles were attached large iron rings, for the convenience of the shipping moored there. The outermost of those piles having a ring was called *ring's end*, that is, *the end*, or *last of the rings*; and hence the name given to the place at the end of Sir John Rogerson's-quay. Sir John Rogerson, the maker of the quay, was at one time [1693-4] Lord Mayor of Dublin; and my information as to the derivation of the name *Ring's End* was received from old Jemmy Walsh, a Dublin pilot, who remembered seeing the ships moored, and their ropes run through the rings of the wooden piles on the river."

The foregoing is quoted merely to be refuted in the words of another correspondent, who well observes (2nd S., iv. 298) that " Ringsend was so called for generations before ' old Jemmy Walsh ' was born. His derivation, fanciful as it is, I could almost imagine was given to try how far Irish wit could impose on English credulity."

Mr. Lascelles, in " Liber Munerum," &c., Part V., p. 142, writes as follows:—

" *Ringsend* or *Rinksen* [*forsan* a northern word, signifying a sewer, which the river Dodder is to that part of the county.]"

However, the derivation given in the text is probably the correct one, namely, *Rinn-Aun*—"the point of the tide." In fact, the name of Ringsend, as in the case of the Phœnix Park, is a corruption of an Irish word or words, for which a more familiar English one resembling it in sound was substituted. Bishop O'Brien, it may be added, gives in his " Irish-English Dictionary" (Paris, 1768), "*Abhan*, a river; rectius *Amhan*"; and remarks, that the names of places in Ireland with a similar beginning (Rinn) would more than fill a sheet.

Note (ee), p. 22.

THE PIGEON-HOUSE AND THE LIGHT-HOUSE.—From the " Point " of Ringsend, the South-wall extends into the bay 17,754 feet; nearly three English miles and an half. It was commenced in 1748, and finally completed in 1796; and is composed of blocks of mountain granite, strongly cemented, and strengthened with iron cramps. The breadth of the road to a strong artillery station called the Pigeon-house (which was erected near the close of the last century, and is 7,938 feet from Ringsend), is nearly forty feet, and thence to the Light-house thirty-two feet at bottom, but narrows to twenty-eight feet at top; the whole rising five feet above high-water. There is a basin at the former place, 900 feet long by 450 broad, and a landing-place raised 200 feet broad, on which are several convenient wharfs, now but little frequented. The pier at this point is 250 feet wide; and on it are raised buildings, which were formerly used as a magazine, an arsenal, and a custom-house. In the channel between the Pigeon-house and the Light-house is the anchorage called Poolbeg (formerly denominated Cleer-rode, Clareroad, and Clarade) where vessels may lie in fifteen feet at low water. At the extremity of the Wall is the Light-house, commenced in 1761, and completed in 1768, under considerable difficulties, by Mr. Smith. See Whitelaw and Walsh's "History of Dublin," Vol. II., p. 1084; Brewer's "Beauties of Ireland," Vol. I., p. 178; and D'Alton's "History of the County of Dublin," p. 853. Woodcuts of the Light-house and the Pigeon-house are given in the *Dublin Penny Journal*, Vol. III., p. 281; and a view of the Light-house in "Illustrations of the Scenery and Antiquities of Ireland," Vol. I., p. 104.

In an interesting and authentic MS. in the writer's possession, entitled "Observations made by Colonel [afterwards Major-General] Roy during a Short Tour in Ireland, 1766" (see *Notes and Queries*, 2nd S., vii. 358, 442), the following passage occurs :—

"If at any time hence it should be thought necessary to build a fort or citadel near Dublin, the sandy point where now the village of Ringsend stands would seem to be a proper situation to make choice of, as it would effectually secure the entrance of the harbour, in some degree command the bay, might always be supplied by sea, and being overlooked by nothing, might therefore be made strong, especially by means of the little river Dodder. The tide might be made to flow round it."

The Pigeon-house Fort was subsequently erected, and formed, in the plans of Robert Emmet in 1803, one of his chief points of attack. See Dr. Madden's "Life and Times of Robert Emmet," pp. 89, 110, 127.

Note (ff), p. 22.

KING JAMES'S VISIT TO RINGSEND.—" Sir Cloudesly Shovel came on the 12th to Belfast, as convoy to several ships that brought over necessaries for the army; and there having intelligence of a frigate at anchor in the bay of Dublin, and several other small vessels loaden with hides, tallow, wools, some plate, and several other things designed for France, he sailed April the 18th (being Good Friday), to the mouth of the bay of Dublin, and there leaving the Monk, and some more great ships, he took the Monmouth yacht, and one or two more, with several long-boats, and went to Polebeg [Poolbeg], where the frigate lay (being one half of the Scotch fleet that was taken in the Channel the year before), having sixteen guns and four pattereroes. King James when he heard it, said, It was some of his loyal subjects of England returning to their duty and allegiance; but when he saw them draw near the ship, and heard the firing, he rid out towards Rings-end, whither gathered a vast crowd of people of all sorts, and there were several regiments drawn out, if it were possible, to kill those bold fellows at sea, who durst on such a good day perform so wicked a deed (as they called it). Captain Bennet that commanded the frigate, run her on ground, and after several firings from some other ships of theirs, as also from that, when they saw a fireship coming in (which Sir Cloudesly had given a sign to) they all quitted the frigate, being at first about forty; but they lost six or seven in the action. Sir Cloudesly was in the Monmouth yacht where Captain Wright was very serviceable both in carrying in the fleet, and in time of action. In going off, one of our boys ran a-ground, and was dry when the tide was gone; the rest of the boats were not far off, being full of armed men; and a Frenchman, one of King James's Guards, coming nigh the boats to fire his pistols in a bravo, had his horse shot under him, and was forced to fling off his jack-boots and run back in his stockings to save himself; some of the sea-men went on shore, and took his saddle and furniture. When the tide came in, they went off with their prize to the ships below. King James went back very much dissatisfy'd, and 'twas reported he should say, That all the Protestants in Ireland were of Cromwell's breed, and deserved to have their throats cut: but whatever his thoughts might be, I suppose his discretion would not allow him to say so. However all the Protestants that walked that way during the action, were secured in prison, and two made their escape to our boats."—Story's "Impartial History of the Wars of Ireland," p. 58.

Note (gg), p. 23.

RINGSEND CARS. — "The hackney-coaches we borrowed from our English neighbours, as their name imports; but our one-horse vehicles have always been peculiar to ourselves, and were in use long before anything of a similar kind was introduced into England. The earliest and rudest of these were the 'Ringsend cars,' so called from their plying principally to that place and Irishtown, then the resort of the *beau monde* for the benefit of sea-bathing. This car consisted of a seat suspended in a strap of leather, between shafts, and without springs. The noise made by the creaking of the strap, which supported the whole weight of the company, particularly distinguished this mode of conveyance." ("Sketches of Ireland Sixty Years Ago," p. 77.) See also Whitelaw and Walsh's "History of Dublin," Vol. II., p. 1173. This "History" may not be particularly well arranged; but containing a great mass of useful information, and very little extraneous matter, it is oftentimes too hastily condemned.

Note (*hh*), *p.* 23.

MONUMENTS IN IRISHTOWN CHURCH. — In the church there are four small-sized monuments—

I.

" In remembrance of Elizabeth, the beloved wife of Colonel Munro, Royal Artillery. She died in Dublin, 20th December, 1843."

II.

" Sacred to the memory of John Babington Smyth, M.D., Belmont House, Stillorgan. Born in 1822; Died September 27th, 1845.

" ' Ποία γὰρ ἡ ζωὴ ὑμῶν; ἀτμίς.'—JAMES, iv. 14."

III.

" To Robert Hanna, A.B., T.C.D. This tablet was erected by his pupils in the Rev. Dr. Wall's School. He died Oct. 25th, 1848, aged 23 years."

IV.

" S. M. of John Smyth, A.M., M.D., T.C.D., of Belmont House, Stillorgan, Co. Dublin. Esteemed by his acquaintances, endeared to his friends, beloved by his family, through a life of varied usefulness his path was that of the just, ' as the shining light that shineth more and more unto the perfect day.' Released from his labours, he rested with his Redeemer, December 4th, 1852."

Mr. D'Alton, in his " History of the County of Dublin," p. 857, enumerates several, besides those mentioned in the text, who have been interred in the churchyard, and whose tombstones may be found. Accurate copies of many of the inscriptions, for which there is not room here, are in the writer's possession.

Annals of the Parishes.

[Many particulars recorded in the preceding pages are here repeated, or referred to, in chronological order.]

The following early mention of this part of Ireland may prove interesting to the reader:—

A.M.

2820. "The Annals of Clonmacnoise, after detailing the migration of Parthalon from Greece to Ireland, thus describe the plague which destroyed his colony on the plain of Dublin:—269 years after its arrival, when 'all that then remained alive of them, to the number of 9,008 persons, from the first Monday in May untill the next Monday after, died of a sudaine infection, upon the plaine of Moynealta. It was called Moynealta, because all the foule in the kingdom for the most part gathered themselves there to sun themselves.' This plain of Magh-Nealta must have included the strand of Clontarf, the mouth of the Liffey, and as far as Blackrock, along the shore, and extended back into the old plain of the flocks, stretching along the valley of the Liffey, and southward to Tallaght." — "Report of the Census Commissioners" (1851), Part V., vol. i. p. 41.

A.D.

1173. Richard (Strongbow) Earl of Pembroke gave Dovenalbroc (Donnybrook), with other lands, to Walter de Riddlesford, Baron of Bray.—Rot. in Canc. Hib.

1178. About this time Archbishop O'Toole confirmed the townland of Simmonscourt, *inter alia*, to the cathedral of Christ Church.

1192. In the charter of King John (then Lord of Ireland) to the city of Dublin, the river Dodder is mentioned as the "Dother," and its course from Donnybrook to the sea prescribed as a part of the boundaries of the liberties of the city. See *Note* (m).

12—. Pope Innocent III., in the beginning of the thirteenth century, confirmed to St. Patrick's Cathedral the tithes of the land in Donnybrook previously granted by King John to the citizens of Dublin.

1204. King John granted to the corporation of Dublin license for an annual eight-day fair at Donnybrook, commencing on the day of the finding of the Holy Cross (3rd May), with similar stallages and tolls as established in Waterford and Limerick. The greater part of the lands of Donnybrook were at this date the property of Henry de Vernuil. (Rot. in Turr. Lond.) See *Note* (y).

1228-55. The church of Donnybrook, dedicated to St Mary, and (as appears from an award of Archbishop Comyn, 1181-1212) a member of Tancy, was for a time disunited therefrom, and conferred by Archbishop Luke upon his chaplain, William de Romney. The same prelate afterwards reduced it to the condition of a chapelry, and made it subservient to Tancy, and consequently to the archdeaconry of Dublin.—Repert. Virid. Alani.

1234. Between 1186 and this year, the priory of All-Hallows received, with other grants, forty acres of land in the territory of Dovenachbroc (Donnybrook) towards the north; the Canons to pay yearly 1lb of pepper for pottage. This pound of pepper, and all hereditary rights belonging to the land, were afterwards assigned by John de Hoethe, jun., to Sir Robert Bagod.

1252. King Henry III., by charter, extended the duration of Donnybrook Fair to fifteen days, and changed the day of its commencement to the 7th of July; which was further altered to the 10th of the same month, and by a subsequent charter fixed to the 26th of August.

1280. Soon after the Invasion, "the rath near Dovenadbroc" was given to Theobald Walter, the first Butler; and in 1280 the manor of "Rath" was granted to Sir Robert le Bagod, with the water of the Dodder hence to the sea, and the commons of the woods of Maynooth. This grant, however, was contested by the Butlers down to the year 1320. (Rot. in Canc. Hib.) The above-named Sir Robert granted to the nunnery of St. Mary de Hogges three acres of Bagotrath, as it was then called, in exchange for a messuage and curtilage in the suburbs of Dublin, belonging to said nunnery; the Prioress thereof also rendering to him and his heirs a pair of gloves, or threepence, in lieu of all services. For some particulars of this nunnery, &c., see Gilbert's "History of Dublin," vol. iii. p. 2.

13—. In the fourteenth century the Fitzwilliam family were seised of a carucate in Donnybrook, but the manor was in the Powers; one of whom, Eustace le Poer, aliened it to the Archbishop of Dublin without the royal license, but was pardoned on account of his great services against the O'Byrnes and other Irish enemies in Leinster.—Rot. in Canc. Hib.

1331. In this and the foregoing year, when a grievous famine afflicted all Ireland, the citizens of Dublin received, about the 24th of June, an unexpected relief at the mouth of the Dodder, where a prodigious number of large fish called Turlehydes were cast ashore. "They were from thirty to forty feet long, and so bulky, that two tall men placed one on each side of the fish could not see one another. The Lord Justice, Sir Anthony Lucy, with his servants and many of the citizens of Dublin, killed above two hundred of them, and gave leave to the poor to carry them away at their pleasure" (Harris's "History of Dublin," p. 265). These Turlehydes, or Thurlheads, were probably the species of cetacea known as the bottle-nozed whale. We read in Stow's "Chronicle," under A.D. 1532, that two great fishes called Hurlepooles (probably the same description of animal) were taken in the Thames; and in A.D. 1552 they are styled in the same work Whirlepooles. See "Report of the Census Commissioners" (1851), Part V., vol. i. p. 84.

1373. On the occasion of convening the great council to be held in Dublin, the Sheriff was directed to summon, with others, John Cruys, of Meryon.

1374. By a royal mandate of this year, William Fitzwilliam was removed from the custody of the manor and castle of Bagotrath, which had been the property, as the writ recites, of William Bagot, and the same were committed to the Bishop of Meath. (Rot. in Canc. Hib.) From this time the Bagot family have had no connexion, save in the name, with this locality.

1389. In this year William Fitzwilliam and John Cruys, with others, were appointed Guardians of the Peace in the county of Dublin; with which authority the former was solely invested in 1391.

1392. By writ reciting an ordinance of Parliament, to prevent merchants from buying up for the foreign markets falcons, "austercos vel trecellos," in Ireland, John Cruys, of Meryon, was appointed to inquire into any violation of the order. (Rot. Pat. in Canc. Hib.) This member of the Cruise family was then seised of the manors of Merrion, Thorncastle, Kilsallaghan, &c.; very soon after which the former two passed to the Fitzwilliams.

1394. In this year, and in 1397, William Fitzwilliam was Sheriff of the county of Dublin, and had the custody of the Staines ("between the site of the present College-grounds and the sea"), in order to preserve the watercourse free and clean for the benefit of the citizens. He died in 1397.

1399. By a writ reciting that, whereas John Cruys, "chevaler," who had been summoned to a great council in 1394, held 160 acres at Thorncastle, the rent of which to the Crown he was unable to discharge, by reason of the premises being subject to be burned and laid waste by adjoining Irish enemies of the mountains, it was thereupon directed that he should be exempted from any such payments during his life. An inquisition of 1407 finds that he died seised, in his own right and in right of his wife, of the manors of Merrion, etc., of which Thomas, their son and heir, afterwards became possessed.

1403. Sir Edward Perrers and Johanna, his wife, obtained a grant of Bagotrath, stated to be within the liberties of Dublin, and to be thenceforth held of the Mayor and Commons of that city.—Rot. in Canc. Hib.

1408. Henry Fitzwilliam and two more, by royal mandate, were directed to levy "smok-silver" (i.e., one penny for each house through which smoke passed) over the county of Dublin.

1418. The Prior of All-Hallows was seised of certain lands and tenements in Donnybrook and Baldoyle. — King's MSS.

1420. King Henry V. granted to Hugh Burgh the custody
of the manor of Thorncastle, and all its appurtenances in
Merrion, Ballyboother, Donnybrook, and elsewhere, in the
county of Dublin, as lately held by James Fitzwilliam,
deceased.

1432. Richard Fitzwilliam was living at Donnybrook in
this year.

1442. Philip Fitzwilliam, presumed to be the son of the
above-named Richard, was living at Meryong at this
date; and in 1446, being one of the Counsellors to Richard
Duke of York, had a remittal of all the chief rent he was
to pay the King, during life. Henry VI. granted him a
sum of money out of the crown-rents, which he was to
pay for his manor of Thorncastle, in order to enable him
to rebuild a fort there, which had been destroyed by the
Irish in 1437.

1488. By an act of the Parliament of Drogheda, in which
the bounds of "the four obedient shires," constituting the
Pale, were traced, the following relates to Dublin :—
" From Merryon, inclusive, to the water of the Dodder, by
the new ditch to Saggard, Rathcoole, Kilhell, Rathmore,
and Ballymore, &c. Thence to the county of Kildare,
into Ballycutlan, Harristown, and Naas ; and so thence to
Clane, Kilboyne, and Kilcock, in such manner that the
towns of Dalkey, Carrickbrennan, Newtown, Rochestown,
Clonken, Smethistown, Ballyboteer (Booterstown), with
Thorncastle and Bullock, were in Dublin-shire."

1488. The form of "riding the franchises," as the same was
done on the 4th September in this year, taken from the
White Book of Christ Church, is given in Whitelaw and
Walsh's " History of Dublin," vol. i. pp. 95-98.

1511. Thomas Fitzwilliam, of Meryon, Brey, and Bagotrath, was Sheriff of the county of Dublin, in 1511 (3
Henry VIII.), and is proved by inquisition to have died
in 1529.

1535. Sir Nicholas Fitzwilliam (third son of William Fitzwilliam, of Meryon) was Treasurer of St. Patrick's Cathedral ; which dignity he held until its suppression in
1546, when he was granted by King Edward VI. a
a pension for life of £66 13s. 4d., Irish.

1538. In a list of the lands and possessions of the late dis-

solved monastery of All-Hallows, which remains in the
Chief Remembrancer's Office, mention is made of "forty
acres of land with their appurtenances in Donabrook."—
Whitelaw and Walsh's "History of Dublin," vol. i.
p. 412.

1542. Sir Thomas, son of Richard Fitzwilliam, had livery of
seisin of all the manors, &c., of Dundrum and Thorncastle, and all messuages and other possessions in Dundrum, Thorncastle, Ballybot (Booterstown), and Ovenis-
ton. For some particulars of him, see Archdall's "Lodge's
Peerage of Ireland," vol. iv. p. 312.

1546. At the time of the dissolution of St. Patrick's Cathedral, which happened in this year, the Archdeacon of
Dublin had, with other tithes, those of Donabroke, extend-
ing over the townlands of Donabroke, Meryon, Smothes-
cort, Baleschatter, the lands of All-Hallows, and Bagotrath,
besides a mansion and three stangs of arable land. His
(William Power's) possessions being confiscated in like
manner with those of the other members of the Chapter,
the parish of Donabroke was leased to John Sharpe (Rot.
Pipæ). "Donabroke demesne," belonging to the Rector,
was worth 3s. 4d. per annum; and the tithes, together
with the tithes of fish, alterages, and oblations (besides
the Curate's stipend and repair of the chancel), £15:
total, £15 3s. 4d.—Monck Mason's "History of St.
Patrick's Cathedral," p. 46.

1565. Sir Henry Sydney, Lord Deputy, having landed at
Dalkey, proceeded the next morning to the house of
Thomas Fitzwilliam, of Meryon, whence he made his solemn entry into Dublin.—Harris's "History of Dublin,"
p. 35.

1578. Sir Thomas Fitzwilliam, of Bagotrath and Meryon,
had a grant of the monastery of Holmpatrick, with its
possessions therein fully detailed, including eight cottages,
131A. arable, 12A. meadow, 18A. pasture and furze, and
the custom of the said cottages in the town of Holmpatrick, being the demesne-lands of said priory, &c. He died
9th November, 1592.

1580. Henry Usher, D.D., was in this year appointed
Archdeacon of Dublin, and consequently Rector of Donnybrook, &c. In 1595 he became Archbishop of Armagh;
but continued to hold the archdeaconry in *commendam*,

until his death in 1613. Donnybrook, therefore, was held for twenty-three years by one of the Primates of all Ireland.

1582. A grant of certain dues of the port of Dublin for eighty-one years, by lease from the Corporation, was made to Nicholas Ball, in consideration of which he was to build a tower at Ringsend, like Maiden Tower in Drogheda, and to keep perches in the river.

1592. Sir Richard Fitzwilliam, of Meryon, who succeeded his father in this year, was Constable of the castle of Wykynglow (Wicklow), and Lord Warden of the marches of Leinster, in the reign of Queen Elizabeth; and brought two archers on horseback to the general hosting at Tarah, 24th September, 1593. He died 5th March, 1595, being seised of Bagotrath, &c.

16—. A Manuscript Book of Obits in Trinity College, Dublin (F 4, 18), contains links of the pedigree of the O'Maddens, of Bagotrath, through six generations of the 16th and 17th centuries.—D'Alton's " King James's Irish Army List," p. 519.

1602. The form of " riding the franchises," as the same was done this year, is given in Whitelaw and Walsh's " History of Dublin," vol. i. pp. 98–103. " The modern manner of surveying and perambulating the city liberties every third year" is given in pp. 103–105. See also *Notes and Queries*, 2nd S., viii. 295.

1605. To Sir William Ussher, of Donnybrook, and his son, Arthur, was granted, 28th June (3 James I.), the office of Constable of the castle of Wicklow, and of the other places to said castle belonging: which office " had been granted on 16th Feb., 39 Eliz., to William Ussher, who surrendered same, and prayed that it might be granted to him and his son."—Erck's " Repertory of Patent Rolls of Chancery," vol. i. p. 261.

1610. Sir Thomas Fitzwilliam, of Meryon, who had succeeded his father in 1595, and was knighted in 1608, suffered a recovery of Booterstown, two messuages, and 140A, &c.; all which he held of the King *in capite*.

1615. The regal visitation of this year reports the rectory of Donnybrook as appertaining to the archdeaconry of Dublin, and that the church and chancel were in good repair.

E

1618. "James Crelie, of Newrie, drowned in the Harboroughe of Dublin, about the Ringsende," 2nd April.—Funeral Entries, Ulster Office, vol. iii. p. 73.

1628. Arthur Ussher, of Donnybrook, elder son and heir of Sir William Ussher (jointly with whom he had been appointed Clerk of the Council General of Ireland in 1603), was "drowned in Donabrook river" (the Dodder), of Monday, 2nd March. — Dan. Molyneux's MSS. in Trinity College, Dublin (F. 3, 27, p. 14).

1629. Sir Thomas Fitzwilliam, created Viscount Fitzwilliam, of Meryon, and Baron Fitzwilliam, of Thorncastle, 5th August, with the annual creation fee of £13 6s. 8d., payable out of the customs of the port of Dublin. The patent for his English earldom, granted in 1645, was not perfected.

1635. Nicholas Fitzwilliam, of Holmpatrick and Balldungan, in the county of Dublin, died 5th December, and "was buried with his ancestors in the church of Donnybrooke."

1640. An act of Parliament was sought, for confirming the possessions of the Dean and Chapter of Christ Church in Simmonscourt; but it was resisted by the Lord of Merrion, as prejudicial to his right in a moiety of said lands in fee-simple by ancient inheritance, and in the other moiety by lease. The proposed bill was thereupon thrown out.

1642. Sir Simon Harcourt marched against the castle of Carrickmayne (Carrickmines), to dislodge its Irish garrison. He was shot in the attack, and died the following day at Lord Fitzwilliam's house in Merrion, whither he had been with difficulty removed.—Borlase's "History of the Irish Rebellion," p. 97 (Dublin, 1743).

1646. The Parliamentary forces landed at Ringsend, 14th November.

1649. According to Boate's "Ireland's Natural History," p. 60 (London, 1652), Mr. John Ussher, father of Sir Wm. Ussher, though in the presence of many of his friends on both sides of the river, was drowned in crossing the Dodder. But there must be an error in this statement, Alderman John Ussher (to whose munificence and religious zeal we owe the publication, in 1571, of the first book ever printed in the Irish language, and who was Sir

William's father) having died 1st May, 1600. (Elrington's " Life of Archbishop Ussher," Appendix 1, p. x ; and Gilbert's " History of Dublin," vol. i. p. 382.) Arthur Ussher, Sir William's elder son, was drowned in the Dodder, as already stated, in 1628.

1649. In the immediate vicinity of Ballsbridge, and on the right of the road from Dublin, stood Bagotrath Castle, which was seized during the night by the forces of the Marquess of Ormonde, on his meditated investiture of the city in this year; but soon after daybreak the next morning, the assailants were driven out by the garrison of Dublin, and completely defeated. In 1651 the Castle was taken by storm by Oliver Cromwell. All remains of it have long since disappeared; and within the last few years several handsome houses have been erected on its site.

1649. Oliver Cromwell, Lord Lieutenant of Ireland, landed at Ringsend, 14th August, with 8,000 foot, 4,000 horse, a formidable train of artillery, and all other necessaries of war. Here Henry Cromwell also subsequently landed. " Upon his arrival in the bay of Dublin, the men-of-war that accompanied him, and other ships in the harbour, rung such a peal with their cannon, as if some great good news had been coming to us; and though the usual landing for those who came in ships of war was near my house [at Monkstown], yet he and his company went up in boats to the Ringsend; where they went ashore, and were met there by most of the officers, civil and militiary, about the town."—Ludlow's " Memoirs," vol. ii. p. 86 (Edinburgh, 1751).

1650. About this year the first bridge over the Dodder at Ringsend was erected, when it singularly occurred, that the bridge was scarcely finished, and a safe passage effected over this heretofore dangerous stream, than it suddenly altered its channel, leaving the bridge on dry ground and useless; " in which perverse course," says Boate, " it continued, until perforce it was constrained to return to its old channel, and to keep within the same."—" Ireland's Natural History," p. 60.

1654. A survey of this date represents " Butterstown " as containing 240A., of which 200A. were arable, 35A. pasture, and 5A. meadow, the property of Sir William Reeves, of Rathsallagh, an English Protestant, by virtue of a mortgage from the Lord of Merrion, " an Irish papist;" that there was on the grounds a castle in repair; that the premises were a manor, with courts leet and baron; and that the tithes belonged to Christ Church.

1654. A survey of this date states that Merrion had been the property of the Lord of Merrion; that the premises were an old decayed castle and an extensive burrow; that said premises constituted a manor, with courts leet and baron; and that the tithes belonged to the College of Dublin.

1654. A survey of this date makes Simmonscourt to contain 110A., of which 80A. were arable, 20A. meadow, and 10A. pasture; that it had been the property of the Lord of Merrion; and that the tithes belonged to the College of Dublin.

1657. Sir William Ussher, of Donnybrook, Clerk of the Council, died in this year, though Lewis, in his " Topographical Dictionary of Ireland," vol. ii. p. 516, falling into the error of Messrs. Whitelaw and Walsh, makes him to have been drowned in the Dodder in 1649. In his house in Dublin, in 1602, had been printed the first Irish version of the New Testament. See Gilbert's " History of Dublin," vol. i. p. 385.

1660. At this time, the Archdeacon of Dublin's glebe in Donnybrook was one park and three stangs, demised to Mr. William Scott.

1663. Oliver, second Viscount Fitzwilliam, of Merrion, created Earl of Tyrconnel by patent, dated 20th April, 1663; or rather 1661, as we find him Earl of Tyrconnel 29th July in that year, and 9th July, 1662, he took his seat by proxy in the House of Peers.—Lords' Jour. i. 274, 317.

1664. " Ringsend and out-Liberties," as stated in an old MS. document in the writer's possession, relative to Hearth-Money in Dublin, 1664–5, were charged £16 10s. for 165 chimneys.

1666. In a grant of 178A. statute measure, part of Simmonscourt, to the Earl of Tyrconnel, the rights of the Dean and Chapter of Christ Church were especially saved.

1666. His Majesty's patent, bearing date 8th June, 1664, and containing a gracious pardon to the Earl of Tyrcon-

nel for all crimes, treasons, &c., committed before the 29th
December, 1660, in relation to any war in England and
Ireland, and a clause of restitution to his estate, having
been confirmed, he passed patent accordingly, 11th July,
1666, for Ringsend, Merrion, &c.; and that year made a
settlement thereof to the use of himself and his Countess
Eleanor, for their respective lives; remainder to their heirs
male; remainder to his brother William for life; remainder to Thomas, son of the said William, and his heirs
male; with other remainders over.—Archdall's "Lodge's
Peerage of Ireland," vol. iv. p. 317, n.

1667. Oliver Earl of Tyrconnel buried in the churchyard of
Donnybrook, 12th April. See *Note (bb)*. The earldom
became extinct; but in his other titles he was succeeded
by his brother William, third Viscount Fitzwilliam, of
Merrion, who died before the year 1681, and was succeeded
by his only son Thomas. The King granted to the Earl's
widow an abatement of quit-rents and a pension of £300
a year for life.

1670. A great storm happening at new moon, in the month
of March, the tide overflowed the banks of the Dodder at
Ringsend, flooded up to the College, and very high into
the city; some houses were swept down, and many cellars
and warehouses laid under water.

1670. John Lord Berkeley, Baron of Stratton, Lord Lieutenant of Ireland, landed at Ringsend, 21st April.

1674. Proposal made to form a harbour at Ringsend.—Yar-
ranton's "England's Improvement by Sea and Land,"
pp. 151-155 (London, 1677).

1684. The glebe of Donnybrook defined in a lease of this
date, as adjoining the churchyard on the north side, and
containing half an acre.

1690. King James II. visited Ringsend. See *Note (ff)*.

1691. December 5th, when De Ginckel was departing for
England, the Lords Justices, and most of the nobility and
gentry in and about Dublin, accompanied him to Ringsend.—Story's "Impartial History of the Wars of Ireland," Part ii. p. 288.

1697. About this time the corporation of Dublin conveyed
their right of holding a fair at Donnybrook to the Ussher
family.

1698. "Abram le Grove executed and hung in irons below Ringsend, for a horrid murder he committed on a Dutch skipper," 7th February.—"Chronological Remembrancer."

1703. The inhabitants of Ringsend having become numerous by the accession of many officers of the port, seamen, and strangers, and being not only distant from Donnybrook, their parish church, but prevented from resorting thither by tides and waters overflowing the highway, an Act was passed, on the application of the Archbishop and Archdeacon of Dublin, authorising Thomas Lord Viscount Merrion to convey any quantity of land, not exceeding two acres, for a church and churchyard for their accommodation; and the Archbishop was empowered to apply £100 out of the forfeited tithes towards building same. (2 Anne, c. xi. s. 8) The endowment afterwards took effect in the adjacent village of Irishtown Strangely enough, almost every one who has written about Irishtown Church, has stated that it was built "for the use of the garrison of Pigeon-house" (or in such like words); whereas, though the exact date of its erection is not known, the former building preceded the latter by little less than a century.

1704. Thomas, fourth Viscount Fitzwilliam, of Merrion, who had been outlawed as a supporter of King James II., but whose outlawry was reversed, died 20th February, and was succeeded by his only son Richard, fifth Viscount, who conformed to the Established religion in 1710, and whose elder daughter Mary was married, in 1733, to Henry Earl of Pembroke.

1709. Thomas Earl of Wharton, Lord Lieutenant of Ireland, landed at Ringsend, 21st April.

1711. About this year, agreeably to a plan suggested by a Mr. Corneille, and also in consequence of an opinion of Captain Burgh, his Majesty's Surveyor-General, a new channel for the river Liffey was made between the city and Ringsend. "While these works were going on, a proposal was made in the year 1713, by Captain John Perry, for the improvement of the harbour: his plan was to make a low wharf or pier of drift-work, from Irishtown to the outermost point of the South Bull, and to make a dam from the Ringsend to the high lands on the north side, to pen the water of the Liffey and Dodder to somewhat above the high water of a spring tide, with a stone

sluice in the embankment to admit vessels into the basin.
This plan does not seem to have been attended to. . . .
It seems, however, pretty evident from the works which
were afterwards carried into execution, that the low pier
of drift-work recommended by him was the principle on
which they proceeded."—" Reports on Dublin Harbour"
(1800–2), p. 63.

1712. The extant parish registers of Donnybrook commence
with this year. The earliest book is entitled " An Ac-
count of the Marriages, Christnings, and Burialls, of the
Protestants [and others] within the Parish of Donebroke,
since March the 27th, 1712. George Fitzgerald, Clerke.
This Book was boght at the Parish-charge. Mr. Patrick
Kelley and Mr. Thomas Freeman, Churchwardens." See
Note (t).

1714. About this year surveys were ordered relative to the
propriety of piling below Ringsend; and in consequence
thereof, the preparatory work was soon after begun, by
sinking wicker-work kishes filled with stones: and in
1717 the piling commenced.

1715. From the following entry in the parish register of
Donnybrook, the Rev. Walter Thomas, who was Curate of
the parish in the same year, would appear to have had
some connexion with St. Matthew's, Ringsend :—" Sep.
1st, 1715, Mr. Lewis bought of the Rev. Walter Thomas
his seat in the Chapple of St. Mathew's in Irishtown,"
etc., for £4. Mr. Thomas was perhaps the Minister of
St. Matthew's before it was endowed in 1723, the yearly
expenses having been defrayed by a tax levied on every
sailor who crossed Dublin Bar.

1716. " Buried, Madam Cleton, in the Chancell of Donebrook," 1st February—[? the mother of Bishop Clayton,
who was buried in 1758.]—*Donnybrook Parish Register.*

1719. " July 27th. It is agreed on between Mr. Thomas
Thomas, of Donebrook, and Mr. Thomas Wilkinson, of
Ringsend, Churchwardens for the ensuing year, dividing
£60 sterling between them, y^t is to say, thirty-seven
pounds sterling on the upper ward or country part of the
parish of Donebrook, and twenty-three pounds sterling on
Ringsend and Irishtown, being the lower ward."—*Donnybrook Parish Register.*

1719. Charles Whittingham, D.D., appointed to the archdeaconry of Dublin in December, 1719, on the resignation of Archdeacon Dougatt; and died in 1743. His name appears in almost every page of the parish register of Donnybrook during his incumbency; and he probably resided constantly in the glebe-house in the village of Donnybrook. This house, situated at one end of Churchlane (which in former days was the resort of many of the *beau monde* of Dublin, and from which was the entrance to the churchyard), was subsequently well known as the Rosetavern, the "Salt-hill" of its day: in later times it degenerated into a public-house; but happily it is once more a private dwelling, though one of an humble character. "Buried, Madam Whittingham, Sept. 13th, 1731."— *Donnybrook Parish Register.*

1723. A King's Letter issued (10 Geo. I.) "for establishing a minister at Ringsend," 23rd May; and the Rev. "John Buherean" (or Boherean, as in the attested copy of his appointment in the possession of the present Chaplain, Dr. Wall) appointed "to the ministry or curacy of the chapel in Ringsend." ("Liber Munerum," Part v. p. 142.) "Buherean" is evidently a misprint for Buhereau, *al.* Bohereau, *al.* Borough; the last being the form of the name on his tombstone. He died in 1726, and (as stated in the parish register of Donnybrook) was buried, 11th May, in the churchyard of St Matthew's, Ringsend. A writer in the *Christian Examiner* (March, 1857) refers to some interesting French MSS., which were placed in Abp. Marsh's Library, Dublin, by the Rev. Elias Bohereau, D.D., Precentor of St. Patrick's Cathedral, and the first Librarian, who died in 1719; and states that he has "heard it asserted that Sir E. Borough [of Dublin] is a descendant of the Rev. Elias Bohereau," who was a French refugee, and whose third son was the Rev. John Borough, of Ringsend. See "Burke's Baronetage."

1726. The Rev. Michael Hartlib (not Isaac Hartlitt, as he is called by Mr. D'Alton), Rector of Killary, or Killarvey, in the diocese of Meath (1703), appointed to the chaplaincy of St. Matthew's, Ringsend, 1st June, on the death of the Rev. John Borough. Mr. Hartlib died in 1741, and was buried in St. Bridget's churchyard, Dublin, 26th August (*Parish Register of St. Bridget's*). His burial is recorded likewise in the parish register of Donnybrook.

1726. The bay of Dublin witnessed a very memorable scene, when Dean Swift, on his return to Ireland in the month of August, was received with all the honours which the "Drapier's Letters" had earned for him, and brought to his landing-place in triumph.

1726. According to Dr. Threlkeld, a broad-leaved variety of the *absinthium maritimum* was found between Merrion and Blackrock. The country people in his time [1726] made the common kind into sheaves, and brought it to Dublin, where it was used in brewing an ale called purl.—"Synopsis Stirpium Hibernicarum," *sub voce.*

1726. Eighteen persons, men, women, and children, drowned near Ringsend, by the oversetting of a boat.—"Chronological Remembrancer."

1728. Mr. John Day, one of the Churchwardens of Donnybrook for this year, was unable to write, as appears from "his mark" in the parish register! His case, we have every reason to believe, was singular.

1728. A reference to Brooking's curious "Map of the City and Suburbs of Dublin," published in this year, will show that very great changes have taken place in Irishtown and the neighbouring districts during the last century.

1729. William King, D.D., Archbishop of Dublin, buried in the churchyard of Donnybrook, on the north side, 10th May. See *Note* (*u*). For some particulars respecting portraits of him, see Bishop Mant's "History of the Church of Ireland," vol. ii. p. 496; or, Wills' "Lives of Illustrious and Distinguished Irishmen," vol. iv. p. 308.

1729. Ringsend-bridge rebuilt.

1730. "Buried, Robert Dougket, Late AD.," 13th August (*Donnybrook Parish Register*). Robert Dougatt, A.M., was appointed to the archdeaconry of Dublin in 1715, which he resigned in 1719; and became Precentor of St. Patrick's, and Keeper of Abp. Marsh's Library, on the death of Dr. Bohereau in that year. He was nephew to Archbishop King.—Cotton's. "Fasti Ecclesiæ Hibernicæ," vol. ii. pp. 112, 130.

1732. "Married [in Donnybrook Church] Jeffery Foot and Jane Lundy, 13th April." Alderman Lundy Foot was baptized 21st April, 1735, and buried 5th January, 1805. —*Donnybrook Parish Register.*

1733. Sir Edward Lovet Pearce, M.P., buried in the church-yard of Donnybrook, 10th December. There also was interred, 20th January, 1738, his brother, the Right Hon. Lieut.-General Thomas Pearce, who "was at once Governor, Mayor, and Representative in Parliament, of the city of Limerick;" and Lady Pearce, 17th July, 1749 (*Donnybrook Parish Register*). See *Note (p)*.

1735. A light-ship, being a small sloop, with a lantern at her mast-head, was placed at the end of the Piles, near to the situation of the present Lighthouse.

1737. "Buried, William Jones, of Brickfield," 24th July (*Donnybrook Parish Register*). In Rocque's "Plan of the City of Dublin and the Environs," published not many years after this date, "Brickfield Town" and the "Conniveing House" appear where Sandymount now is; and in his "Actual Survey of the Environs of the City of Dublin" (first sheet), we find, *inter alia*, "Black Rock Avenue" (now the Cross-avenue); "Merrion Lane" (now Booterstown-avenue) and the "Mass House;" "Lord Merrion's Brick Fields;" and "The Piles," with the Light-ship, &c. These maps contain some curious particulars, and deserve a careful inspection.

1737. William Duke of Devonshire, Lord Lieutenant of Ireland, landed at Ringsend, 7th September.

1740. "The strand in the neighbourhood of Irishtown was famous for the quantities of shrimps caught there; but the great frost of 1740 destroyed them, and the few that are now [1776] found are neither so large or delicate."—*Exshaw's Magazine*.

1740. About this year the factory at Ballsbridge, for printing linen, calico, and cotton, was opened. It was subsequently much extended and improved by Messrs. Duffy & Co.; but for several years past it has been discontinued, and the buildings applied to other uses.

1741. The Rev. Isaac Mann, D.D., appointed to the chaplaincy of St. Matthew's, Ringsend, 4th November, on the death of the Rev. Michael Hartlib. He held at the same time the rectory of Killary, or Killarvey, in the diocese of Meath. In 1757 he became Archdeacon of Dublin; and in 1772 was raised to the bishoprick of Cork and Ross.—Cotton's "Fasti Ecclesiæ Hibernicæ," vol. ii, p. 131.

1742. "Buried, Henry Lord Power, in y⁰ Vault of St. Mathew's Chappel [Ringsend], May 6th" (*Donnybrook Parish Register*). "This individual," as Mr. D'Alton writes, "but for the effect of attainders, was the Lord Power of Curraghmore, and should be commemorated by the Waterford family, who enjoy what were once the estates of the Poers. His name you will find in the Civil Establishment of 1727, for an annuity of £550, although the Irish Parliament had objected to the grant. He had claimed the estate of Curraghmore, as heir male of [James Earl of Tyrone] the father of Lady Catharine Poer, who on her marriage had brought over that property to Sir Marcus Beresford [afterwards created Earl of Tyrone]; but of course he failed in his suit." For particulars of the family, see Archdall's "Lodge's Peerage of Ireland," vol. ii. p. 303. See also *Notes and Queries*, 2nd S., viii. 518.

1742. "Buried, Frances Trotter, in the Cabbage Garden [near St. Kevin's Church, Dublin, and long a favourite place of burial with the Wesleyans], 10th December."— *Donnybrook Parish Register*.

1743. Richard, fifth Viscount Fitzwilliam, of Merrion, who had succeeded his father in 1704, died at Thorpe, in Surrey, 6th June.

1744. "Buried, Governor Richd. Fitzwilliams" (?), 18th May.—*Donnybrook Parish Register*.

1746. Archdeacon Pococke (a learned man and accomplished traveller, and subsequently Bishop of Meath) held a Visitation in St. Patrick's Cathedral, "which perhaps is the latest of such visitations on record in Ireland."

1747. "Buried, Lady Newport," 28th February (*Donnybrook Parish Register*). She was the daughter and coheiress of —— Anderson, Esq., of Worcestershire: and became the wife of Robert Lord Newport, who was Lord Chancellor of Ireland, and twelve times sworn one of the Lords Justices, and died "in the government," 3rd December, 1756, having been advanced to the dignity of Viscount Jocelyn in the preceding year. Lady Newport died 23rd February, 1747, being the mother of Robert, afterwards first Earl of Roden. In the same register is recorded the burial, 16th July, 1762, of Lieut.-Colonel George Jocelyn, who was wounded at the battle of Fontenoy in 1745, was appointed Deputy-Governor of Carlisle,

and died at Leixlip, unmarried, 14th July; and also that
of John Jocelyn, Esq., an officer in the army, who died
suddenly in Dublin, 16th December, 1765, aged 45, and
was buried two days after "in the family-vault at Irishtown."—Archdall's "Lodge's Peerage of Ireland," vol. iii.
pp. 268, 269.

1748. "Buried, July y*e* 23, Lord Mayo's Son" (*Donnybrook
Parish Register*). This was Sir Aylmer Bourke, only
son of John, eighth Viscount Mayo, by Catharine, daugh-
ter of Major Whitgift Aylmer, descended from Dr. John
Aylmer, Bishop of London, and from Dr. John Whitgift,
Archbishop of Canterbury, both in the reign of Queen
Elizabeth. He was born 17th November, 1743; died
21st July, 1748; and two days after "was buried in the
church of Irishtown, near Dublin."—Archdall's "Lodge's
Peerage of Ireland," vol. iv. p. 249.

1748. Henry Ussher granted several denominations of land
at Donnybrook, together with the Green, to Catherine
Downes, in fee, excepting and reserving unto said Henry
Ussher, his heirs and assigns, the benefit and profit of
holding the yearly fair in the usual place. Ulysses de
Burgh, Lord Downes, is the present proprietor in fee of the
ground.

1748. The South-wall, nearly three English miles and a-half
in length, commenced in this year, and finally completed
in 1796. It was carried as far as the site of the Pigeon-
house within the first seven years. See *Note* (*ee*).

1750 Proposals were issued in Dublin for publishing an
English, Irish, and Latin Dictionary, by a Mr. Crab, of
Ringsend; but the book was never printed. "Finding
its way into the library of the late General Vallancey, it
was purchased, when his books were sold, at the price of
forty guineas, for a gentleman of Irish birth, the Rev.
Dr. Adam Clarke" (Anderson's "Sketches of the Native
Irish," p. 98). Is this to be identified with "General
Vallancey's Gælic Dictionary," 2 vols., folio? These volumes were sold in 1836, on Dr. Clarke's death, for
£52 10s., to Mr. Thorpe, of London; being "one of the
most important manuscripts on the ancient Irish language
extant, and on which the indefatigable and enthusiastic
author spent upwards of thirty years." The annexed note
is from the inside of the cover of the first volume:—

"Bought against the Dublin University and the kingdom of Ireland, at the sale of General Vallancey's books, in 1813, for £57, by me, A. C."

1750. The Very Rev. Theophilus Brocas, A.M., Dean of Killala, appointed to the chaplaincy of St. Matthew's, Ringsend, 4th December, on the resignation of the Rev. Dr. Isaac Mann. He held it until 1764; and dying in 1770, was buried in St. Anne's Church, Dublin.

1750. A survey of about this date, makes the Archdeacon of Dublin's glebe in Donnybrook to contain 2 roods, 24 perches, besides a garden of 24 perches between it and the churchyard, doubted whether part of the glebe or not : the churchyard itself measures 1 rood, 8 perches.

1751. Hires of coaches for set-downs from Dublin to Blackrock, 2s. 2d.; Butterstown, 2s. 2d.; Donnybrook, 1s. 1d.; Merrion, 2s. 2d.; Mount Merrion, 2s. 2d.; and Ringsend, 1s. 1d. " No more to be demanded if they return immediately, or in ten minutes. Otherwise, to have 6½d. by the hour, over the time spent in going and returning." Hires of Ringsend cars or chaises for set-downs from Dublin to Blackrock, 9d.; Butterstown, 9d.; Donnybrook, 3d.; Merrion, 9d.; Mount Merrion, 9d.; and Ringsend, 3d. " They are to have 3d. by the hour over and above the time spent in going and coming. Or for waiting, 6d. the first hour, and 3d. every hour after. And a British half-crown for the whole day."—" Watson's Almanack."

1753. "The Lord Mayor, attended by several of the city officers, went to Donnybrook [Monday, 20th August], where his Lordship issued a proclamation forbidding any person to erect tents or booths there till the Fair-day appointed by patent, and to take them down and disperse at the end of the day, on pain of incurring such penalties as the law directs in case of disobedience."—*Universal Advertiser*, 25th August.

1753. The Very Rev. Robert Watts, D.D., "Dean of Ossory" (more correctly, Dean of Kilkenny, or Dean of St. Canice), buried 20th December (*Donnybrook Parish Register*). See Cotton's " Fasti Ecclesiæ Hibernicæ," vol. ii. p. 291.

1754. It is set forth in a return made this year by the Rev. Thomas Heany, of Monkstown, relative to the parishes of Monkstown, &c., that " two third-parts of the Blackrock and Booterstown tythe, although in the parish of Donnybrook, belong to the Dean of Christ Church, and one-third to the Curate of Monkstown. The tythe of fish belongs to the Curate, and is usually set at the yearly rent of £5." See *Note* (*d*).

1754. "The damage, occasioned by the heavy rain this day [14th June] and the preceding night, exceeds anything of the like nature that can be remembered. A few instances out of many will be sufficient to evince the melancholy truth. . . . the Paper-mill at Ballsbridge, together with Mr. Grant's improvements, and a large quantity of stamped linens, were born away by the current."—*Universal Advertiser*, 18th June.

1754. "We hear a subscription is set on foot for building convenient bathing places at the Blackrock, for the accommodation of such as resort thither for the benefit of the water."—*Universal Advertiser*, 23rd July.

1756. On the death of Henry Ussher in this year, the right of holding Donnybrook Fair became vested in Sir William Wolseley, Bart., who in 1778 made a lease thereof to Joseph Madden, of Donnybrook; and in 1812 the then Baronet absolutely assigned same for ever to John Madden, son of the aforesaid Joseph, by the representatives of whom, and of his brother Peter, the same was sold in 1855. See *Note* (*y*).

1758. Robert Clayton, D.D., Bishop of Clogher, buried in the churchyard of Donnybrook, 1st March. See *Note* (*s*). "Cathren Clayton, ye Bp.'s wife," buried in same place, 8th January, 1766.—*Donnybrook Parish Register*.

1758. As would appear from advertisements in *Sleater's Public Gazetteer* of this year, Donnybrook and Ballsbridge linens, printed by Messrs. Thomas Ashworth and Co., were in great demand. Mr. Ashworth's name frequently appears in the parish register.

1759. Bartholomew Mosse, M.D., the founder of the Dublin Lying-in Hospital (the first establishment of the kind in her Majesty's dominions), buried in the churchyard of Donnybrook, 18th February. See *Note* (*q*).

1759. It has been said that the Archdeacon of Dublin has a dormant power of granting marriage-licenses within his archdeaconry; and the following entries in the parish register of Donnybrook tend to confirm the idea :—"Married by the Archdeacon's License, by the Rev. Michael Heatly, Mr. Charles Christian to Mrs. Mary Lovett, 24th May, 1759"; and, "Married by the Archdeacon's License, Mr. Henry Hopley to Mrs. Jane Brown, by the Rev. Dr. Mann, Archdeacon of Dublin, 19th February, 1764."

1761. The foundation of the Lighthouse in Poolbeg, near Dublin Bar, laid. In Scalé and Richards' "Directions for Navigating into the Bay of Dublin," etc. (Dublin, 1765), p. 22, it is stated that " as the Light-house on the Piles is not finished, the Light-ship continues to display her ensign from half-flood to half-ebb in the day, and her lanthorn's-light from half-flood to half-ebb in the night." The Light-house finished in 1768, under considerable difficulties, by John Smith, Esq. See *Note (ee).*

1761. George Earl of Halifax, Lord Lieutenant of Ireland, landed at Ringsend, 6th October; and embarked at same place for England, 1st May, in the following year.

1762. " Buried, Rev. Dr. John Winn," 21st January (*Donnybrook Parish Register*). This was the Rev. John Wynne, A.M., Precentor of St. Patrick's Cathedral, and " Keeper of [Archbishop Marsh's] the publick Library of Dublin."

1763. "Married, the Hon. William Beresford to Miss Elizabeth Fitzgibbons," 12th June (*Donnybrook Parish Register*). The Hon. and Rev. Wm. Beresford, brother of the first Marquess of Waterford, was appointed to the see of Dromore in 1780, and translated to Ossory in same year. In 1794 he became Archbishop of Tuam ; and having been created Lord Decies in 1812, died in 1819. Miss Elizabeth Fitzgibbon was the second daughter of John Fitzgibbon, Esq., a barrister of eminence, who had a house close to Donnybrook-green ; and the sister of the subsequently well-known Earl of Clare.—Cotton's " Fasti Ecclesiæ Hibernicæ," vol. iii. p. 285, iv. p 18 ; and Archdall's " Lodge's Peerage of Ireland," vol. ii. p. 309.

1763. A violent storm of wind and rain, which did much damage to the shipping at Poolbeg, 25th September. Two new houses in Ringsend blown down.—*Freeman's Journal.*

1763. In the rental of the estate of All-Hallows, taken from the rental of the estate of the city of Dublin, as it was in this year, and printed in Harris's "History of Dublin," p. 492, William Ussher, Esq., appears as tenant of land near Donnybrook, at the annual rent of £100.

1764. The Rev. John Brocas, A.M. (likewise Dean of Killala from 1770), appointed to the chaplaincy of St. Matthew's, Ringsend, 29th March, on the resignation of the Very Rev. Theophilus Brocas. He died in 1795.

1764. "Yesterday their Excellencies the Lords Justices, attended by the Lord Mayor, Sheriffs, and Committee of Directors of the Ballast Office, were graciously pleased to go in barges down the water, to visit the South-wall, the Cassoon, and the new Light-house erecting for the security of this harbour. . . . Their Excellencies were pleased to accept of a cold repast provided for them and their friends at the Block-house, and expressed their approbation of the conduct of these great works, to the great satisfaction of the Committee."—*Freeman's Journal*, 11th August.

1764. Donnybrook Parish charged at this date with Minister's Money to the amount of £60.—*Freeman's Journal*, 2nd October.

1765. Died "at Mount Merrion, near this city, aged 112 years and 3 months, Francis Jones, by trade a brogue-maker. He retained his senses to the last, and never lost a tooth." —*Freeman's Journal*, 4th May.

1765. "Our High Sheriff, attended by the proper officers, a strong guard, and about twenty-five cars, went to Donnybrook [31st August], and caused the tents to be pulled down; with which the cars were loaded, also with pots, tables, forms, &c., and brought to the Tholsel. The tents were pulled down the day before, but daringly erected again, notwithstanding the orders given to the contrary. In all probability much mischief would have been done, if the vigilance of the Sheriff had not put a stop to the continuing the Fair."—*Freeman's Journal*, 3rd September.

1766. "Married, by Consistory Licence, by the Rev. Thomas Heany, Capt. Charles Vallancey, Esq., to Mrs. Julia [?] Blosett," 15th Jan., 1766.—*Donnybrook Parish Register*.

1766. The Rev. John Leland, D.D., a Presbyterian minister in Dublin, and author of "A View of Deistical Writers" (first published in 1754), and of other works, buried 19th January.—*Donnybrook Parish Register*.

1766. A house at Ringsend taken by the Governors of the Hibernian Nursery for the Marine. (*Freeman's Journal*, 28th June.) The funds and the number of the boys increasing, ground was taken at the lower end of Sir John Rogerson's-quay, and the present building opened in 1773.

1776. Richard, sixth Viscount Fitzwilliam, of Merrion, who had succeeded his father in 1743, died 25th May, and " was interred in Donnybrook-Chapel."

1782. For some particulars of these parishes, see " A Tour through Dublin and its Environs, in 1782," in *Walker's Hibernian Magazine* for 1783, p. 239.

1782. " About two in the morning [16th August] the most dreadful fall of rain began in Dublin and its neighbourhood that was ever remembered in that country ; it continued for fourteen hours with a violence that was truly alarming; the distress of the inhabitants of Dublin is beyond description. Ringsend-bridge [erected in 1729] was borne down by the flood." (*Annual Register*.) It was not until 1786 that statutory enactments were passed for restoring the communication, and supplying Ringsend and Irishtown with water from the Dodder.

1784. Great floods in Dublin and its neighbourhood, caused by the overflow of the Liffey, Dodder, and Poddle watercourse, 3rd January.—*Walker's Hibernian Magazine.*

1786. Fort Lisle (now Elmcliff), Blackrock, was at this date, and for some years after, the residence of John Lysaght, Lord Lisle. Lisaniskea, which adjoins, was then called Elmcliff.

1787. In this year occurred one of those remarkable floods, by which the Dodder has been so frequently affected. " Ringsend was in a very melancholy situation. It resembled a town which had experienced all the calamities of war, that had been sacked by an enemy, or that had felt the hand of all-devouring time. The unfortunate inhabitants were in a manner excluded from all intercourse with Dublin. They were attacked by the overbearing floods, which issued from the mountains in irresistible torrents, and completely demolished the bridge. The new bridge [as in 1796] is a very handsome one, and cost only £815."—Ferrar's " View of Dublin," &c., p. 74.

1789. The Duke of Wellington's first victory. See *Note* (*w*).

F

1790. For some fond allusions to Irishtown at this date, see "Life of Theobald Wolfe Tone," vol. i. p. 35.

1790. Sir Jonah Barrington gives in his "Personal Sketches,". vol. iii. pp. 230-259, an amusing, but very questionable, account of his visit in this year to Donnybrook Fair.

1791. Cranfield's Baths, situated on Irishtown-strand, and said to be the earliest public baths in Ireland, opened by Mr. Richard Cranfield, who "shut out the sea, and made land [many years known as Scal'd Hill] from Irishtown to Sandymount." He died there, 24th December, 1859.

1791. A bridge of three arches erected over the Dodder at Ballsbridge. Rebuilt in 1835.

1791. "Died at Donnybrook the Right Hon. [Wm.] Lord [Viscount] Chetwynd." (*Dublin Chronicle*, 15th November.) His "principal country residence" was close to Donnybrook-green.

1792. An inundation of the sea, which made several breaches in the South-wall, and laid all the low grounds between Sir John Rogerson's-quay and Ringsend-bridge under water, 24th January.

1792. The Hospital for Incurables, which had been established in 1743, transferred from Townsend-street, Dublin, to Donnybrook. See *Note* (x).

1793. Died on the Donnybrook-road, 23rd July, the Hon. Robert Hellen, one of the Justices of the Court of Common Pleas. ("Anthologia Hibernica," vol. ii., p. 78.) He was one of " the characters which figure in ' Baratariana '."—*Notes and Queries*, 2nd S., viii. 21.

1793. Miss Anne Keon, of St. Stephen's-green, Dublin, left, with many other large legacies, £1,000 to the Hospital for Incurables.—"Anthologia Hibernica," vol. ii. p. 155.

1794. The Hon. Richard Power, one of the Barons of the Exchequer, having been ordered by Lord Clare to appear in the Court of Chancery, of which he was Usher, and to answer certain charges, threw himself into the sea from the South-wall, near the Pigeon-house, and perished, 2nd February. See Daunt's "Personal Recollections of O'Connell," vol. ii. p. 145 (an amusing book); and Gilbert's "History of Dublin," vol. iii. p. 290.

1794. A portion of Bagotrath Castle, much frequented by
robbers, was standing in this year, a view of the ruins
being given in Grose's "Antiquities of Ireland," vol. i.
p. 10; but not a vestige of them remains.

1794. " Last Wednesday night [17th December] the house of
Lady Barry, at Sandymount, near Ballsbridge, was broken
into by a gang of miscreants, and robbed of valuable arti-
cles to a considerable amount. These savage ruffians, on
entering into Lady Barry's chamber, fired a pistol at her,
which fortunately missed its aim, but strewed the room
with the slugs with which it was loaded."—" Anthologia
Hibernica," vol. iv. p. 477.

1795. When his Excellency Earl Fitzwilliam was leaving
Ireland, 25th March, his carriage was stopped in College-
green by the populace, who took out the horses, and drew
it from thence to the Pigeon-house, where he embarked.
" His Lordship was accompanied by nearly every dignified
character at present in the metropolis, whose carriages
formed a line beyond precedent extensive."—*Newspaper
paragraph.*

1795. The Rev. Robert Ball, LL.B., appointed to the chaplaincy of St. Matthew's, Ringsend, on the death of the
Very Rev. John Brocas. Mr. Ball died in May, 1828,
having held likewise the prebend and vicarage of Drumholm, in the diocese of Raphoe, and was buried in the
churchyard of Stillorgan, 15th of same month.

1795. " Riding to Ringsend, we were presented with a striking proof of the vast extent of human labour and human
genius in the docks building there; and we were highly
pleased to find Counsellor Vavasour reclaiming the great
tract of waste ground near the bridge. . . . At
Sandymount we found a very convenient salt-water bath,
erected by a Mr. Cranfield. . . . To ride over the
extensive strand from hence to Booterstown, added an in-
describable gaiety to our spirits. . . . Going to the
county of Wicklow, the road to the Blackrock is evidently
the pleasantest, most frequented, and level. At Booterstown the fields are disposed in a style of judicious hus-
bandry. The villas are neat and commodious, particularly Lord Carleton's [Willow Park], Mr. White's, Mr.
La Touche's [Sans Souci], Mr. D'Olier's [Collegnes], Mr.
Alexander's [Seamount], and Sir Boyle Roche's, and

denote the neighbourhood of a large commercial city. . .
. . . Williamstown is adjoining Blackrock, and has
been much improved by Counsellor Vavasour" (Ferrar's
"View of Dublin," &c., pp. 74–76). Frescati, near Blackrock (then belonging to the Duchess of Leinster, but subsequently a well known boarding-school, and now divided
into four dwelling-houses), was about this time a favourite resort of Lord Edward Fitzgerald.

1795. Willow Park, Booterstown, had been erected by, and
(as already stated) was at this time the residence of, Hugh
Lord Carleton, Chief Justice of the Court of Common
Pleas. He was created a Viscount in 1797; and having
resigned office in 1800, died in London, without issue, 25th
February, 1826. See the *Gentleman's Magazine* for 1826,
Part i. p. 270, where is given a just tribute to his character from Duhigg's "History of the King's Inns" (Dublin, 1806).

1795. If John Sidney Taylor, who became well known for
"his maintenance of the principles of constitutional liberty,
Christian morality, and successful exertion in advocating
the abolition of the punishment of death," was not born
about this year in his father's house in Donnybrook, he
certainly passed there some of his early days.

1796. The corporation for improving the port of Dublin,
with the view of helping to clear the channel of the Liffey,
diverted the Dodder from its natural bed (which ran
through the ground on which the Rev. Dr. Wall's houses
are built) into a new channel through the low grounds
between Irishtown and Dublin.

1796. Mr. Benjamin Higgins was the author of a very interesting "Account of the Rise and Progress of the Lying-
in Hospital in Dublin, with an Attempt towards the Life
and Character of Doctor Bartholomew Mosse," which appeared (almost in full, and for the first time) in the *Dublin
Quarterly Journal of Medical Science*, November, 1846.
Mr. Higgins held the registrarship of the Hospital; and
at a meeting of the Governors, 14th May, 1796, it was
"resolved, that this Board will place a tombstone in the
churchyard of Donnybrook, over the grave of the said
Benjamin Higgins, as a lasting [?] testimony of their
regret at his loss, and of their grateful sense of his unremitting zeal for this institution."

1797. " This day [28th August] the Lord Mayor and his attendants perambulated the franchised boundaries of Dublin. When they arrived at the strand of Booterstown, the tide being at the lowest ebb, his Lordship, from the water's edge, threw a dart into the sea. The spot where it fell was noted as the extreme of the municipal jurisdiction, according to ancient custom."—*Newspaper paragraph.*

1798. " Detachments from the U.C. Fusileers and St. Sepulchre's Infantry seized some arms in the environs of Merrion-avenue," 2nd April.—*Idem.*

1798. " Last Sunday [27th May] the whole of the male inhabitants of Williamstown, and most of those of Blackrock, Newtown, Dunleary, and Monkstown, went voluntarily before the Magistrates, and took a strong and solemn oath of allegiance to his Majesty, and against associating with United Irishmen, or any unlawful society. And on Tuesday the whole of the inhabitants of Williamstown entered into resolutions, declaring their readiness to take up arms in defence of their king and country, and the laws of the realm, against any traitors or conspirators."—*Idem.*

1798. " This morning [1st June] a body of about 500 or 600 persons, inhabitants of Ballsbridge, Donnybrook, and their vicinities, repaired to Sandymount, there to take the oath of allegiance before Alderman Truelock," who, in the month of October following, being in a state of mental derangement, shot himself in his house at Simmonscourt. —*Idem.*

1799. " We are sorry to observe that the Magistrates of Dublin are so inattentive to its peace as to suffer the continuance of that annual nuisance, Donnybrook Fair, so many days beyond the time for which it has unfortunately a legal claim to exist. . . . . The Fair continued until yesterday, and will probably last until it shall grow into such an enormity of riot and outrage as shall cure itself."—*Faulkner's Dublin Journal,* 3rd September.

1799. " Napper Tandy and his associates landed yesterday evening [18th November] at the Pigeon-house, from the Loftus packet, and were conveyed to Kilmainham goal. Tandy was clad in a white serge wrapper, resembling a friar's gown, and wore a very large hat, turned up with a loop on one side."—*Newspaper paragraph.*

1800. King George III. granted a charter of incorporation to "the Governors and Guardians of the Hospital for Incurables, near the City of Dublin," 7th January. See "Report of Commissioners appointed to inspect Charitable Institutions, Dublin" (1824), pp. 118-135.

1800. The Rev Gore Wood, who had been for many years Curate of the parish, buried in the churchyard of Donnybrook, 25th May.—*Donnybrook Parish Register.*

1800. Bloomfield, Merrion, was at this date the country residence of John Ball, Esq., M.P. for Drogheda, who "in his progress to the highest professional eminence never stooped to any unworthy condescension," and "though the ablest lawyer of his day, was passed over in all Lord Clare's promotions." A plain serjeant-at-law, he died 24th August, 1813. "By the unanimous vote of the Irish Bar," a monument was erected to his memory in St. Patrick's Cathedral, Dublin; and another by the corporation of Drogheda, in St. Peter's Church, in that town, where he was buried. See Monck Mason's "History of St. Patrick's Cathedral," Appendix, p. lix.; Phillips' "Specimens of Irish Eloquence," p. 300; Barrington's "Rise and Fall of the Irish Nation," p. 393 (Paris, 1833); and D'Alton's "History of Drogheda," vol. i. p. 35, &c.

1802. In this year the late Sir Thomas Fowell Buxton, Bart., was placed under the care of the Rev. John Moore, Master of Donnybrook School; and in the following year he entered the Dublin University, where his career was particularly brilliant. See *Notes and Queries*, 1st S., vii. 452.

1802. "Donnybrook Fair has been long complained of as a nuisance, and a most dangerous one it is; as the recruiting service is at an end, that excuse can no longer be used," &c.—Dutton's "Observations on Archer's Statistical Survey of the County of Dublin," p. 56.

1802. Captain Huddart has given in his Report on Dublin Harbour, presented in this year to the Directors-General of Inland Navigation of Ireland, an historical sketch of the works carried on for the improvement of the harbour, during the past century, at a very great expense ("Reports on Dublin Harbour," pp. 62-80). Amongst other things, he proposed to extend the South-wall 770 yards, and to erect a new Light-house, at a cost of £155,660.

For a biographical sketch of Captain Huddart, distinguished as a geographer and mechanist, see the *Annual Register* for 1816, p. 220.

1802. Early in December an inundation destroyed the bridge at Ringsend, whereupon was erected the present one of mountain granite, which is supposed capable of resisting any force of water. At this time the number of wherries here was returned as seven.

1803. In the plans of Robert Emmet (who had a depot at Irishtown, in charge of a timber merchant, Mr. Thomas Brangan, residing in that village), the Pigeon-house was a chief point of attack. He "was frequently at Brangan's; and on several occasions they walked across the strand, when the tide was out, to take plans of the Pigeon-house, and make observations." (Dr. Madden's "Life and Times of Robert Emmet," p. 110.) See also p. 1/7 of same work, wherein is given a copy of Emmet's own statement of his plans and intentions. The writer has an interesting MS. (pp. 60), in which frequent reference is made to the Pigeon-house, entitled "Lord Hardwicke's Vindication against the Calumnies of General Fox, Commander of the Forces in Ireland, which attributed the most lethargic indifference, on the part of the Irish Government, to the projected Insurrection of 1803;" and which was drawn up for the perusal of the Cabinet.

1805. John O'Neill directed by his will, that whoever should enjoy a certain interest in the lands of Simmonscourt, should pay, during the continuance thereof, one guinea yearly to the support of Townsend-street Chapel, Dublin.

1807. "Having escaped from the plucking of the Pigeon-house, I am safely lodged upon one of the quays of the Liffey."—Milner's "Tour in Ireland," p. 6.

1807. Ground taken for the College Botanic Gardens, near Ballsbridge.

1807. "Sandymount, 19th October, 1807. I certify that I did this day, at one o'clock in the afternoon, marry Doctor Patrick Duigenan to Mrs. Esther Hepenstal, widow, at Sandymount, in the parish of Donnybrook, and county of Dublin, in the presence of the Rt. Honble. John Monck Mason and sundry other persons. Chars. Dublin [Earl of Normanton]" (*Donnybrook Parish Register*). For a biographical sketch of the Right Hon. Patrick Duigenan, LL.D., who died 11th April, 1816, see the *Gentleman's Magazine* for that year, Part i. p. 871.

1807. The Prince of Wales packet wrecked at Dunleary, and the Rochdale transport at Blackrock, 19th November. See *Note* (cc).

1811. Frescati School, Blackrock, was at this time, and for many years after, under the direction of the Rev. Robert Craig, A.M., who put forth the following advertisement:— " Frescati, 16th Jan., 1811. Mr. Craig, having learned with much concern, that the rumour of an intention to offer himself a candidate for the Mastership of Drogheda School has been industriously circulated, thinks it his duty publicly to state, that such an idea never once entered his contemplation." There were several schools, as appears from the newspapers of this year, in the vicinity of Blackrock.

1811. Aldborough Lodge, opposite Peafield, Blackrock, was at this time the residence of John Earl of Aldborough.

1811. The Roman Catholic Chapel of Booterstown erected, at the expense of Richard, seventh Viscount Fitzwilliam, of Merrion, who had succeeded his father in 1776. The French editor of " The Letters of Atticus" has written of Lord Fitzwilliam, that " a native of Ireland [born 30th July, 1745], where he had very large estates, he expended six thousand pounds sterling in building, in a parish of his domains, a Catholic Church, and took a pleasure in superintending the labours of the workmen." The foregoing statement may not be strictly correct in every particular.

1812. The registers of baptisms and burials in St. Matthew's, Ringsend, commence with this year, being very imperfect until 1818. The parochial clergymen discharged the " occasional duties" until 1812, when Mr. Wogan (who was murdered near Ballsbridge in 1826) declined to do so ; and therefore reference for baptisms and burials in this quarter previous to 1812 should be made to the registers of Donnybrook.

1814. The Rev. Matthew West, A.M., Rector of Clane, in the diocese of Kildare, buried in the churchyard of Donnybrook, 13th September. Mr. West had been Curate of the parish of Donnybrook for some years, and published a volume of poetry; and was " a gentleman whose impressive eloquence as a preacher, and cultivated talents as a scholar, were highly and deservedly appreciated by all who were acquainted with him."

1815. The Rev. George Molden, Assistant-Chaplain, buried in the churchyard of St. Matthew's, Ringsend.

1816. Richard Viscount Fitzwilliam died in London, 4th February, being succeeded in his titles (with an annuity) by his brother John, eighth and last Viscount Fitzwilliam, but leaving his large estates to George Augustus Earl of Pembroke and Montgomery, with remainder to the present Right Hon. Sidney Herbert and his heirs male. Playfair, in his " British Family Antiquity," vol. v. pp. 38-44, gives a very high character of Lord Fitzwilliam, with particulars of his family. See also, for notices of his death, munificent bequests to Cambridge University, &c., the *Gentleman's Magazine* for 1816, Part i. pp. 189, 367, 627; and the *Annual Register* for same year, p. 213. Though he lived and died a Protestant, he was the reputed author of a remarkable, and rather scarce publication, entitled " The Letters of Atticus" [" or, Protestantism and Catholicism, considered in their comparative Influence on Society "], which, having been written in French, and published at different times, were collected and reprinted in London, anonymously, in the year 1811. Another edition appeared in Paris in 1825; and in the following year, in London, an English translation, with Lord Fitzwilliam's name on the title-page.

1816. Erasmus Smith's Schoolhouse, near Donnybrook, for boys and girls, erected. The late Lord Downes, of Merville, and the late Dr. Perceval, of Annfield, gave each £100; about three-fourths of the amount being soon after vested in Government Stock for the benefit of the schools, in the names of the Archdeacon of Dublin and two others. Here the parish of Taney (in which are Donnybrook Cottage, the residence of the late Hon. Judge Plunket, Beechhill, and Beaver-row) adjoins the village of Donnybrook.

1817. The first show of flowers by the Horticultural Society held in Erasmus Smith's Schoolhouse, Donnybrook.

1818. " The Grand Duke Michael, from a wish probably to see society under all its forms, visited this scene [Donnybrook Fair] on Thursday se'nnight [27th August], and was much gratified with the amusements, which the Irish editor is careful to tell us, were as usual ' knocks down for love,' and cut heads, with the never-failing accompaniment of picking pockets. The Irish editor thinks these diversions a certain remedy against treasons, stratagems, and spoils. We are sorry to differ from such high authority; but we really think, from his showing, that Donnybrook Fair is no better a school for virtue than that abominable nuisance which is now infesting Smithfield."—*Newspaper paragraph.*

1818. In the Appendix, No. V., to Whitelaw and Walsh's "History of Dublin," published in this year, a list of the "Salaries of the Officers of the Customs in the Port of Dublin" is given, including the following items:—" Ringsend, four surveyors, each £200; forty-four tide-waiters, each £80; fifty five super. ditto, each £60; two coxswains, one carpenter, and eleven boatmen, each £50; curate of Ringsend, £200; surgeon for sick and wounded officers, £100; clerk of the King's yard, Ringsend, £120, house and allowance."

1818. "The want of churches is much felt and complained of in this neighbourhood [of Monkstown], where there is a more numerous population of the Established religion than in any other part of Ireland. Yet, with the exception of Stillorgan, this [at Monkstown] is the only church from Ringsend to Bray, the extremity of the county, an extent including eleven populous villages, and a very thickly inhabited country."—Whitelaw and Walsh's "History of Dublin," vol. ii. p. 1272, n.

1820. Leonard MacNally, barrister-at-law, whose name is now too well known in connexion with Irish affairs in 1798, buried in the churchyard of Donnybrook, 8th June. A false report of his death, with age and other particulars, having appeared in the newspapers (probably in consequence of the death of his son Leonard, who was buried in Donnybrook, 17th February), the following note (kindly supplied by Wm. J. Fitzpatrick, Esq., of Stillorgan) was sent to the proprietor of *Saunders's News-Letter:*—" Sir— I am advised, from the severe injury I have received in consequence of the great circulation your paper gave of my death on the eve of the Assizes, and my practice in the City of Dublin, to apply to the calm determination of

a City of Dublin Jury for damages against yon.—Your
obed. St., Leonard MacNally. 20, Cuffe-street, Mon.
6 March, 1820."

1821. The population of the parish of Donnybrook, including
Booterstown, amounted to 9,219 ; comprising 4,267 males
and 4,952 females. See *Notes* (*j* and *aa*).

1821. The parish of Booterstown formed out of the parish
of Donnybrook. See *Note* (*d*).

1822. Mr. John Macnamara, formerly of Coolnahella, in the
county of Clare, and latterly of Sandymount, buried at
St. Matthew's, Ringsend. He had been a well-known
collector of Irish MSS., which were again dispersed on his
death. Mention of his MSS. is made in almost every
page of O'Reilly's " Chronological Account of Irish
Writers" (Dublin, 1820).

1823. The Hon. William Fletcher, one of the Justices of the
Court of Common Pleas, resided at Montrose, near Donnybrook, and died in this year.

1824. Miss Hannah Green, of Donnybrook-road, buried in
the churchyard of Donnybrook, 27th April, having left by
will a sum of money for charitable purposes, with which
Government Stock was purchased, amounting to £115 7s.
" The bequest was not specific, but to be applied in charity
in the best manner ; and the late Commissioners of Cha-
rities having received the amount from her executor in
the year 1828, directed that the interest should be given
to the Archdeacon of Dublin, as Incumbent of Donnybrook, in which parish testatrix died, to assist in the
purchase of coals."—*Official information*.

1824. Booterstown Church consecrated and opened for Divine
service on Sunday, 16th May. See *Note* (*a*). The Rev.
James Bulwer appointed to the incumbency. The parish
registers of baptisms and marriages commence with this
year. There is no graveyard, and consequently no register of burials. Searches for baptisms, &c., previous to
this year should be made in the registers of Donnybrook
(of which parish Booterstown was a part) or Monkstown.

1825. The Rev. Anthony Sillery, A.M., appointed to the
incumbency of Booterstown, on the resignation of the
Rev. J. Bulwer. He resigned in 1832. See *Note* (*h*).

1826. Died at his seat, Merville, Stillorgan-road, 3rd March, in his 75th year, the Right Hon. William Downes, 1st Baron Downes, and late Chief Justice of the Court of King's Bench. He had been born in Donnybrook Castle, which was subsequently a well-known boarding-school, and is now a nunnery; and was the son of Robert Downes, Esq., of Donnybrook, M.P. for the county of Kildare, by Elizabeth (married 18th Feb., 1737), daughter of Thomas Twigg, Esq., likewise of Donnybrook. (*Gentleman's Magazine* for 1826, Part i., p. 270; and "Burke's Peerage.") Merville (like Mount Merrion, Seafield, and Trimleston, in the parish of Taney, but on the confines of Booterstown) has been for some years past the residence of Lieutenant-General Hall, C.B.

1826. The Rev. George Wogan, who had been for twenty-six years Curate of Donnybrook, murdered in his house in Spafield-place, near Ballsbridge, 21st April, and buried two days after in Donnybrook churchyard, aged 70 years. The same tombstone covers the remains of three who had been clergymen of the parish, but without any inscription. Denis Hynes and George Stanley, both of Booterstown, having received sentence of death for a highway robbery committed the same night on the Blackrock-road, confessed the murder, and were hanged. See Donnybrook Vestry-book, pp. 22, 52, for full particulars.

1826. Booterstown Schoolhouse, Cross-avenue, erected, at an expense of nearly £700. "Sept. 5, By Cash from Treasury, £184 3s. 1d." appears in the account.

1827. St. Mary's Church, Donnybrook, erected at Simmonscourt, the foundation-stone having been laid by Archdeacon Torrens. In the parish accounts there appears a charge of £6 for a silver trowel. The building was not opened for Divine service until 1830. See *Note* (*k*).

1828. As appears from the vestry-book of the parish of Booterstown, "Mrs. Easterby" and "Miss Kells" attended the vestry held on Easter Monday, 7th April. In the same book may be found many particulars respecting the parish, from 20th July, 1821.

1828. The Rev. John Evans Johnson, A.B. (now D.D., and Archdeacon of Ferns), appointed to the chaplaincy of St. Matthew's, Ringsend, in May, on the death of the Rev. Robert Ball.

1828. For an account of His Excellency the Marquess of Anglesey's visit to Donnybrook Fair on Saturday, 30th August, see the *Freeman's Journal*, 3rd September.

1829. Mary Myers, of Ringsend, buried in the churchyard of St. Matthew's, 21st March, aged 103 years. She had never (as she informed Dr. Wall) slept a night out of Ringsend, which in her youthful days " was very clean, healthy, and beautiful, with vines trained up against the walls of the houses," &c.

1829. The Very Rev. Richard Graves, D.D., Dean of Ardagh, buried in the churchyard of Donnybrook, 3rd April. See *Note (s)*.

1830. St. Mary's Church, Donnybrook, opened for Divine service.

1830. Sandymount Loan-Fund instituted, 1st October.

1831. The Rev. Richard H. Wall, A.M. (now D.D.), appointed to the chaplaincy of St. Matthew's, Ringsend, 22nd April, on the resignation of the Rev. J. E. Johnson, having held the assistant-chaplaincy from 18th October, 1818.

1831. The population of the parish of Booterstown amounted to 3,549; comprising 1,454 males and 2,095 females;—and that of Donnybrook to 10,394; comprising 4,729 males and 5,665 females.

1832. The Rev. Robert H. Nixon, A.M., appointed to the incumbency of Booterstown, in July, on the resignation of the Rev. A. Sillery. He died 22nd January, 1857. See *Note (g)*.

1832. Anglesey-bridge erected over the Dodder at Donnybrook.

1832. Irishtown Schoolhouse completed, at an expense of £800, defrayed by subscription. Ground having been granted by the late Earl of Pembroke, the building was begun in 1824; and after many delays from various causes, a public meeting of the subscribers was held in the vestry of St. Matthew's, Ringsend, 31st December, 1831, when it was unanimously resolved to vest the trust of the building in the Chaplain of St. Matthew's for the time being, for a Protestant male school, an almshouse for Protestants, and a general dispensary.

1833. For a very interesting "story of the last century," entitled "The Pidgeon House," see the *Dublin Penny Journal*, vol. ii. p. 99, published in this year. It was compiled from information supplied by old inhabitants of Ringsend; and gives the history of Pidgeon and his family. "Buried, Richard Pigeon [?], 19th July. 1713" (*Donnybrook Parish Register*). Pidgeon's House, as described in the *Journal*, was succeeded by Tunstall's Tavern, for many years a great resort of the people of Dublin; and no country gentleman, if he had not dined at Mrs. Tunstall's, was considered to have seen the metropolis. The Pigeonhouse Fort, as already stated, was erected towards the close of the last century.

1833. The Schoolhouse (now the Courthouse) in Sandymount-green erected by subscription.

1833. On the death of John, eighth Viscount Fitzwilliam, of Merrion, the honours of the family became extinct. The Rev. Mervyn Archdall, in his edition of "Lodge's Peerage of Ireland," vol. iv. pp. 306-321, gives many particulars of this family, to the year 1789; and a little additional information may be gained from the third issue of "Burke's Extinct and Dormant Peerage" (London, 1846). Playfair likewise devotes some space to the family in his "British Family Antiquity," vol. v. pp. 33-44 (London, 1810). More, however, might well be in print respecting the Fitzwilliams of Merrion.

1834. In the "Second Report on Ecclesiastical Revenue and Patronage, Ireland" (1834), p. 219, John Madden appears as the tenant of a "house and garden near Donnybrook, containing 1 A. 0 R. 8 P.," under a lease for 40 years, of which twenty-three remained unexpired on 29th Sept., 1832. Annual rent, £2 1s. 6¼d.

1834. According to Mr. Wm. Tighe Hamilton's "Abstract of the Census of the Population of Ireland," p. 74, Booterstown Parish contained in this year 980 members of the Established Church, 1,751 Roman Catholics, 19 Presbyterians, and 8 other Protestant Dissenters: total, 2,758. Donnybrook Parish, 3,536 members of the Established Church, 6,712 Roman Catholics, 50 Presbyterians, and 17 other Protestant Dissenters: total, 10,315. See *Notes* (*j* and *aa*).

1834. Ballsbridge Schoolhouse erected in this year, and subsequently enlarged.

1834. The Hammersmith Iron-works, Ballsbridge, established by Mr. Richard Turner.

1834. An inundation of the Dodder in the month of November, whereby a temporary bridge at Ballsbridge was swept away, the neighbouring country flooded, and much injury done to the buildings of the Dublin and Kingstown railway.

1834. The Dublin and Kingstown (now Dublin and Wicklow) railway, running through these parishes, first opened to the public, 17th December.

1835. Died at Herbert House (now Cherbury), Booterstown-avenue, where he had resided for many years, 22nd January, the Right Hon. James Fitzgerald, aged 93. He married, in 1782, Catherine, second daughter of the Rev. Henry Vesey, who was created an Irish Peeress in 1826 ; and well known as "the silver-tongued Prime Serjeant" (1784–1799), was the father of the late, and of the present Lord Fitzgerald and Vesey. For a biographical sketch, see the *Gentleman's Magazine* for 1835, Part i. p. 318. " Bully Egan " had previously occupied the same house.

1835. The present bridge over the Dodder at Ballsbridge erected.

1836. About the middle of August, Dublin was visited by a violent storm, which caused a great inundation of the Dodder, and seriously injured the Dublin and Kingstown railway. For some particulars of the " effects produced by the vicinity of a railroad," as observed about this time in this locality by the Rev. Thomas Romney Robinson, D.D., of Armagh, see the " Proceedings of the Royal Irish Academy," vol. v. p. 287. The observations were made in the (now-vanished) Dodder-bank Distillery, belonging to Mr. Haig.

1838. Close to Anglesey-bridge, near Donnybrook, and in front of St. Ann's (formerly Annfield, for many years the residence of the late Robert Perceval, M.D., whose character is well known), stands a small column with the following inscription:—" MDCCCXXXVIII. Erected to the memory of the late Alderman Arthur Morrisson. As a Christian and citizen, there were few to equal, none to surpass him. He was a sincere friend, charitable, kind, and generous. As Lord Mayor of the City of Dublin, he was respected and esteemed." It may serve perhaps to encourage others, to be told that Alderman Morrisson, when Lord Mayor of Dublin, dined at Annfield with Dr. Perceval, towards whom he had there stood in a very different relation in early life.

1839. The spire of St. Mary's Church, Donnybrook, seriously damaged by the great storm, 6th January, and soon after taken down.

1841. The population of the parish of Booterstown amounted to 3,818; comprising 1,312 males and 2,006 females;— and that of Donnybrook to 9,825; comprising 4,464 males and 5,361 females.

1842. By 5 and 6 Vict. c. 23 ("Local and Personal Statutes") further power was granted "to lease parts of the estates devised by the will of Richard, late Viscount Fitzwilliam, deceased, situate in the city of Dublin, and the neighbourhood thereof," &c. The Act details a large amount of information respecting the Fitzwilliam Estate in these parishes.

1842. The townland of Intake (*i.e.*, "taken in" from the sea), in the parish of Booterstown, and the townlands of Bagotrath, Ballsbridge, Beggarsbush, Clonskeagh, Donnybrooke east and west, Forty-acres, Irishtown, Merrion, Ringsend, Sandymount, and Smotscourt, in the parish of Donnybrook, transferred, by 5 and 6 Vict. c. 96, from the ancient county of the city to the new barony of Dublin.

1843. The Right Hon. John Radcliff, LL.D., buried in the churchyard of Donnybrook, 21st July. See *Note* (*r*).

1845. Mr. and Mrs. Orson, and two children, buried in the churchyard of Donnybrook, 5th February; their bodies having been "found in the ruins of their house [on Dodder-bank, near Donnybrook-green], which was consumed by fire under very mysterious circumstances on the morning of the 3rd instant." (*Donnybrook Parish Register.*) For a full report of the coroner's inquest, see *Saunders's News-Letter*, 6th February.

1846. Ringsend National Schoolhouse for boys and girls, erected by the Right Hon. S. Herbert, opened in January. An Infant School was soon after added.

1846. A violent storm in Dublin, and great floods in the Dodder, 21st November. For particulars of damage done in these parts, see *Saunders's News-Letter* of the 23rd.

1847. Many improvements effected in the old churchyard of Donnybrook, which had been for some years in a very neglected condition. See p. 37.

1849. Queen Victoria, having landed at Kingstown, 6th August, with Prince Albert, the Prince of Wales, and the Princesses, proceeded, by the Dublin and Kingstown railway, to Sandymount-avenue, whence they went through Ballsbridge to Baggot-street, on their way to the Viceregal Lodge. Her Majesty returned by railway to Kingstown, 10th August.

1850. The Church of St. John the Evangelist, Sandymount, opened for Divine service on Sunday, 24th March, as fully reported in *Saunders's News-Letter* of the following morning. The Rev. William de Burgh, A.M. (now D.D.), appointed to the chaplaincy. A view of the building, which cost about £6,000, is given in the *Irish Ecclesiastical Journal*, vol. vi. p. 58.

1851. The Ven. John Torrens, D.D., Archdeacon of Dublin, and Rector of Donnybrook, &c., died at Narraghmore, county of Kildare, 9th June, aged eighty-two years, and was buried in St. Peter's Church, Dublin. A half-length portrait, painted by Middleton, has been engraved by Mr. George Sanders, late of Booterstown.

1851. The Ven. John West, D.D., Archdeacon of Dublin, "read himself in" as Rector of Donnybrook, on Sunday, 3rd August.

1851. The population of the parish of Booterstown amounted to 3,512; comprising 1,336 males and 2,176 females;— and that of Donnybrook to 11,178; comprising 4,971 males and 6,207 females.

1853. The Roman Catholic Chapel of "St. Mary, Star of the Sea," near Irishtown, erected. See "A Letter to the Committee of Management," &c., by William de Burgh, B.D. (Dublin, 1853); and the *Freeman's Journal*, 16th August.

1854. The Right Hon. S. Herbert added to the grounds of Booterstown Church, and made a new and handsome approach from Mount Merrion-avenue.

G

1854. For particulars of the several Parochial Institutions of Donnybrook at this date, see the "Donnybrook Parish Almanack, 1854."

1854. Sunday Evening Service commenced in St. Matthew's, Ringsend, 26th November. See p. 21.

1855. Donnybrook Fair—the Bartholomew of Dublin—abolished, 26th August, in the mayoralty of the Right Hon. Joseph Boyce, the patent having been purchased for £3,000. See *Note (y)*.

1856. London-bridge over the Dodder, near Irishtown, rebuilt, the wooden bridge in same place having fallen into decay.

1857. The Rev. Beaver H. Blacker, A.M., appointed to the incumbency of Booterstown, 18th February, on the death of the Rev. R. H. Nixon.

1858. The Rev. Frederick Fitzgerald, A.M., appointed to the incumbency of Donnybrook, 6th January, the parish having been constituted a perpetual curacy, 1st of same month.

1858. For particulars of the several Parochial Institutions of Booterstown at this date, see the "Booterstown Parish Almanack, 1858." The Almanack was issued likewise for the following year.

1858. The Presbyterian Church, near Irishtown, erected.

1859. The enlargement of St. Mary's Church, Donnybrook, by the addition of a chancel and transepts, commenced in the latter part of this year, under the direction of Joseph Welland, Esq., Architect to the Ecclesiastical Commissioners for Ireland.

Archdeacons of Dublin,

(FROM THE YEAR 1580.)

[For a list of the Archdeacons of Dublin, with particulars, see Cotton's "Fasti Ecclesiæ Hibernicæ," vol. ii. pp. 127–132.]

1580. Henry Ussher, D.D., the first Fellow of Trinity College, and Treasurer of Christ Church, Dublin. In 1595 he became Archbishop of Armagh; but continued to hold the archdeaconry until his death in 1613. See p. 64.

1613. Launcelot Bulkeley, A.M.; became Archbishop of Dublin in 1619.

1619. Anthony Martin, D.D., Prebendary of Castleknock. In 1623 he was likewise Dean of Waterford: in 1625 he became Bishop of Meath; and in 1645 Provost of Trinity College, of which he had been a Fellow.

1625. John Haines.

1636. William Bulkeley, A.M. (son of the Archbishop), Chancellor of St. Patrick's, Dublin (?); died in 1671.

1672. Michael Delaune, A.M.

1675. John Fitzgerald, B.D., late Prebendary of Donoghmore; resigned in 1689.

1690. Dive Downes, B.D., Senior Fellow of Trinity College; became Bishop of Cork and Ross in 1699.

1699. Richard Reader, D.D., Chancellor of Christ Church, and Dean of Emly. In 1700 he resigned the deanery and archdeaconry, and became Dean of Kilmore.

1700. Enoch Reader, D.D., Dean of Kilmore: died in 1709, having held likewise the deanery of Emly.

1710. Thomas Hawley: died in 1715.

1715. Robert Dougatt, A.M.; became Precentor of St. Patrick's in 1719. See p. 73.

1719. Charles Whittingham, D.D.; died in 1743. See p. 72.

1743. Nicholas Synge, D.D., Prebendary of Malahidert, and Precentor of Elphin; became Bishop of Killaloe in 1745.

1745. Richard Pococke, LL.D., Precentor of Waterford, and of Lismore; in 1756 became Bishop of Ossory, and was translated to Meath in 1765. See p. 75.

1757. Isaac Mann, D.D., likewise Precentor of Christ Church; became Bishop of Cork & Ross in 1772. See p. 74.

1772. Edward Bayly, D.D., Dean of Ardfert; died in 1785.

1785. Thomas Hastings, LL.D., Precentor of St. Patrick's; died in 1794.

1794. Robert Fowler, A.M., son of the Archbishop; became Bishop of Ossory in 1813.

1813. James Saurin, A.M., Dean of Cork; in 1818 became Dean of Derry, and Bishop of Dromore in 1819.

1818. John Torrens, D.D., likewise Rector of Narraghmore, in the diocese of Kildare; died in 1851. See p. 97.

1851. John West, D.D., Prebendary of Yagoe, and Vicar of St. Anne's, Dublin. The present Archdeacon.

Incumbents of Booterstown.

1824. James Bulwer, A.M.

1825. Anthony Sillery, A.M.

1832. Robert Herbert Nixon, A.M.

1857. Beaver Henry Blacker, A.M., the present Incumbent.

Incumbent of Donnybrook.

1858. Frederick Fitzgerald, A.M., the present Incumbent.

Chaplain of St. John's, Sandymount.

1850. William de Burgh, D.D., the present Chaplain.

Chaplains of St. Matthew's, Ringsend.

1723. John Bohereau, *alias* Borough.

1726. Michael Hartlib, likewise Rector of Killary, or Killarvey, in the diocese of Meath.

1741. Isaac Mann, D.D., likewise Rector of Killary, or Killarvey, and afterwards Archdeacon of Dublin.

1750. Theophilus Brocas, A.M., likewise Dean of Killala.

1764. John Brocas, A.M., likewise Dean of Killala.

1795. Robert Ball, LL.B., likewise Prebendary and Vicar of Drumholm, in the diocese of Raphoe.

1828. John Evans Johnson, A.B., now D.D., and Archdeacon of Ferns.

1831. Richard Henry Wall, D.D., the present Chaplain.

Churchwardens of Booterstown.

1821. ⎫
1822. ⎬ Robert Alexander and James Digges La Touche.
1823. ⎭

1824. ⎫
1825. ⎬ Robert Alexander and Isaac Matthew D'Olier.

1826. Isaac Matthew D'Olier and Samuel John Pittar.

1827. Robert Roe and Henry Lanauze.
1828. John Elliott Hyndman and Charles Smith.
1829. John Elliott Hyndman and Henry Lanauze.
1830. Hill Wilson and Patrick Stack.
1831. Jonathan Deverell and John Gillman.
1832. Henry Cole and William Henry.
1833. Henry Higinbotham and John Woods.
1834. Isaac Matthew D'Olier and Charles Smith.
1835. Sir J. H. Cairncross, K.C.B., and Hickman Kearney.
1836. Thomas Beasley and Joseph Webster Talbot.
1837. Arthur Ormsby and John Gillman.
1838. Captain J. F. Cockburn and Charles Fletcher.
1839. Capt. William Osborne and Nicholas W. Monsarrat.
1840. James Kelly and Henry Carey Field, M.D.
1841. George Bury and Richard Purdy.
1842. Robert Kelly and Captain Charles Woodward.
1843. Major William St. Clair and Digby Marsh.
1844. Edmund Ball and Charles John Bond.
1845. Captain William Smyth and Edward Browne.
1846. Colonel Joseph Kelsall and Henry Wm. Mulvany.
1847. Captain Richard J. Annesley and Wm. Pennefather.
1848. Hugh Carmichael and James Wright. Captain Annesley, *vice* Wright, resigned.
1849. Edward Browne and David Wilson Hutcheson.
1850.
1851. } Colonel Joseph Kelsall and Joseph Webster Talbot.
1852. John Fitzgerald and George Reade Mac Mullen.
1853. John Maturin and John Fitzgerald.
1854. William P. Alcock and George Reade Mac Mullen.
1855. John Fitzgerald and George Reade Mac Mullen.

1856. George Reade Mac Mullen and Eugene Le Clerc, M.D.
Richard Waring Pittar, *vice* Mac Mullen, deceased.
1857. John Maturin and Henry Loftus Tottenham.
1858. Henry Leland Keily and Edward Clark.
1859. George Charles Armstrong, M.D., and John Reid.

Churchwardens of Donnybrook,

(FROM THE YEAR 1825.)

1825. Francis Thos. Russell and Robert Wright.
1826. Francis Thos. Russell and Daniel Ashford.
1827. Thomas Wright and James Hill.
1828. Capt. Christopher Foss and Thos. Popham Luscombe.
1829. James Jameson and Alderman Thomas Abbott.
1830. Captain C. Foss and Henry D'Anvers.
1831. Charles Tisdall and Crofton Fitzgerald.
1832. Captain C. Foss and Courtney Kenny Clarke.
1833. Crofton Fitzgerald and J. V. E. Cartwright.
1834. Alderman Arthur Morrisson and William Power.
1835. Captain Wm. Loftus Otway and Sir Richard Baker.
1836. Theophilus Page and Captain W. L. Otway.
1837. Robert Corbet and James F. Madden.
1838. John Porter and John Semple, jun.
1839. Captain W. L. Otway and Robert Lovely.
1840. Thomas Bridgford and George M. Walthew.
1841. Henry Humphrys and John Hawkins Askins.
1842. Patrick William Brady and William Henry Murray.
1843. John Hewson and Robert Lovely.
1844. Patrick Wm. Brady and George M. Walthew.

1845. Robert Lovely and Captain William Harris.
1846. John Hewson and Wm. V. R. Ruckley.
1847. Henry Forde and Edward R. P. Colles.
1848. Daniel Kinahan and John Wight.
1849. Captain John W. Welsh and Robert Lovely.
1850. Wm. V. R. Ruckley and James Kildahl Atkin.
1851. John Taylor Hamerton and Henry Humphreys.
1852. Alexander Sanson and James Jameson.
1853. Bartholomew M. Tabuteau and Thos. H. Taylor.
1854. Edward J. Quinan, M.D., and Robert B. Brunker.
1855. Wm. V. R. Ruckley and Francis Salmon.
1856. John Browne Johnston and John Richardson.
1857. Edward Blacker and George Torrance.
1858. Wm. V. R. Ruckley and Edward C. F. Hornsby.
1859. William Henry Morris and John Brereton.

THE END.

www.ingramcontent.com/pod-product-compliance
Lightning Source LLC
Chambersburg PA
CBHW021946160426
43195CB00011B/1242